dead ink

– Liverpool –
MMXXIV

Writing the Murder

dead ink

All rights reserved.

'Introduction' © Dan Coxon & Richard V. Hirst, 2024
'It Bleeds' © Tess Little, 2024
'The Killer Inside Me: Writing the Criminal' © Charlie Higson, 2024
'The Deader the Better: On Writing the Murder' © Andrew Gallix
'Spotlight on... Patricia Highsmith: No Compromises:
The Crime Fiction of Patricia Highsmith' © Barry Forshaw, 2024
'There's Been a Murder: Miscarriages of Justice, Respectability and the Fatal Flaw' © Louise Welsh, 2024
'Setting Out Your Stall' © Carole Johnstone, 2024
'The Mirrored Room' © Saima Mir, 2024
'Spotlight on... Agatha Christie: On Reading as Escape: All of Christie's Murderers, and Me' © Jessie Greengrass, 2024
'Making the Dead Dance: Historical Crime Fiction' © Vaseem Khan, 2024
'Breaking the Translation Barrier' © Quentin Bates, 2024
'Cop Stuff: Fact or Fantasy' © Paul Finch, 2024
'The Method and the Effect: Conjuring the Impossible Crime'
© Tom Mead, 2024
'Spotlight on... Sir Arthur Conan Doyle:
The Problem of the Faithful Pastiche' © Tim Major, 2024

The right of the authors to be identified as the authors of this work has been asserted by them in accordance with the Copyright, Designs and Patents Act 1988.

First published in Great Britain in 2024 by Dead Ink,
an imprint of Cinder House Publishing Limited.

Print ISBN 9781915368737
eBook ISBN 9781915368744

Cover design by Luke Bird / lukebird.co.uk
Typeset by Laura Jones / lauraflojo.com

Printed and bound in Great Britain by Bell and Bain Ltd, Glasgow

www.deadinkbooks.com

Writing the Murder

Essays on Crafting Crime Fiction

Edited by
Dan Coxon & Richard V. Hirst

dead ink

Contents

Introduction — 1

The Means — 7

It Bleeds / *Tess Little* — 9
The Killer Inside Me:
   Writing the Criminal / *Charlie Higson* — 31
The Deader the Better:
   On Writing the Murder / *Andrew Gallix* — 47

Spotlight on… Patricia Highsmith
No Compromises: The Crime Fiction
of Patricia Highsmith / *Barry Forshaw* — 59

The Motive — 73

There's Been a Murder: Miscarriages of Justice,
   Respectability and the Fatal Flaw / *Louise Welsh* — 75
Setting Out Your Stall / *Carole Johnstone* — 97
The Mirrored Room / *Saima Mir* — 109

Spotlight on… Agatha Christie
On Reading as Escape: All of Christie's Murderers,
and Me / *Jessie Greengrass* — 119

The Opportunity 137

Making the Dead Dance:
   Historical Crime Fiction / *Vaseem Khan*   139
Breaking the Translation Barrier / *Quentin Bates*   155
Cop Stuff: Fact or Fantasy / *Paul Finch*   171
The Method and the Effect:
   Conjuring the Impossible Crime / *Tom Mead*   189

Spotlight on… Sir Arthur Conan Doyle
The Problem of the Faithful Pastiche / *Tim Major*   213

Sources   239
Further Reading   245
About the Authors   253
About the Editors   259

Introduction

'There's been a murder.'

It's hard to think of a more evocative – or overused – sentence in the history of crime fiction. It's a sentence underpinned by tragedy and loss, but also by intrigue. It's not simply the case that someone has been killed – they were *murdered*, and within that word lies an entire puzzle box of mysteries to be answered. Who was the murderer? What made them stoop to one of the worst human transgressions? Most importantly: will they get away with it?

Prior to the eighteenth century, if a crime was committed, the responsibility for finding the perpetrator lay largely with the victim and their local community. Watch systems were undertaken, involving residents taking turns to patrol their streets at night, while constables were appointed by local authorities to settle disputes and uphold the law. This changed with the Industrial Revolution, which brought with it urbanisation and populations of ever-increasing density, coupled with widespread poverty. Crime rates surged, necessitating the development of formal police forces to investigate and apprehend offenders. Initially, these forces took on the duties of constables only in larger numbers, their work focused on general law enforcement duties and patrolling.

By the mid-nineteenth century, however, another shift had occurred. The genesis of the detective, as both a literary figure and a real-world profession, can be traced back to the 1840s. This was when Edgar Allan Poe first published 'The Murders in the Rue Morgue', commonly referred to as the first fictional depiction of a detective. In the story, Auguste Dupin, Poe's eccentric but brilliant sleuth, uses observation and deduction to uncover the truth behind the mysterious murder of two women. Around the same time, the London Metropolitan Police appointed the first real detectives, marking a pivotal moment in the evolution in crime detection. Famous murder cases – the Bermondsey Horror, the Road Hill House Murder, Jack the Ripper – made celebrities of the detectives involved: Frederick Field, Jack Whicher, and Frederick Abberline, respectively. Their capacity for logic, undertaken in the fight against humanity's darkest aspects, represented a new era in law enforcement which captured the public imagination.

Little surprise, then, that crime fiction gained significant momentum alongside this development, finding its locus in the 1860s with the advent of sensation fiction and Wilkie Collins's landmark novels *The Woman in White* and *The Moonstone*. Its apotheosis arrived at the turn of the century in the form of crime fiction's two totemic figures – Arthur Conan Doyle and Agatha Christie – who established the genre's key components and crystallised its popularity.

Since then, the cultural status of crime fiction has grown into a dominance. According to Nielsen, more than half a billion crime novels were purchased in the UK alone over the past ten years. This equates to approximately a hundred books purchased every minute of the decade, with public spending on crime fiction totalling £2.5 billion. The genre dominates the book market, with forty per cent of all UK book buyers saying that they read crime novels, a far greater share than any other genre. Indeed, for a large number of readers, crime fiction *is* fiction. A cursory browse through reviews on Amazon will show you that the genre reaches people who engage with little else in the way of literature, and in enviably untold numbers.

This popularity itself presents as something of a mystery, demanding deduction: what is it about crime fiction that continues to hold such sway over us? As we'll see from the following essays, while the English detective novel is considered by many to represent the genre's peak, the genre itself exerts a strong pull across generations, cultures and languages.

It could be contended, as asserted by a number of writers in these pages, that the appeal of crime fiction lies in the satisfaction of solving a puzzle. Alongside the detective protagonist, readers are challenged to piece together a story's clues, anticipate its plot twists, and ultimately unravel its truth. This is reading as an intellectual game, with the cathartic delivery of justice providing a sense of order and control in a world which often feels ruled by chaos and uncertainty.

Alternatively, one could argue, as others in the following essays do, that crime fiction enjoys its popularity because of the opportunity it presents for us to immerse ourselves in the darker aspects of our nature. In our daily lives we rarely experience treachery, violence, murder and consuming guilt. Not only do tales of these things entertain us, they also provide us with a mediated arena where our own fears and anxieties can be dramatised.

Or perhaps the genre's potency lies in its power to do both these things. Crime fiction often appears to embody the essence of storytelling: the interplay of mystery and revelation are the building blocks for any work of fiction. Villains move through the shadowy corridors that run below our collective imagination, pursued by detectives carrying the lantern of truth and justice. We get to dip our toes in dark waters, but safe in the knowledge that someone, somewhere is fighting our corner.

Writing the Murder acts as a scene-of-crime kit for the aspiring crime writer, as well as a resource for those many thousands of crime readers. In 'The Means', Tess Little, Charlie Higson and Andrew Gallix put the genre under the microscope, examining why it enjoys such a lasting appeal and how it weaves its nefarious magic. Then, in 'The Motive', Louise Welsh, Carole Johnstone and Saima Mir confess what it is that draws them to these dark tales of mystery and intrigue – the crime writer's origin story, if you will. Finally, Vaseem Khan, Quentin Bates, Paul Finch and Tom Mead get their hands dirty in 'The Opportunity', as they dissect their chosen subgenres and offer insight into the ways that historical crime, crime in translation, police procedurals and locked-room mysteries capture their readers. Between these sections we shine the spotlight on three key suspects – Patricia Highsmith, Agatha Christie and Sir Arthur Conan Doyle – thanks to the sterling detective work of Barry Forshaw, Jessie Greengrass and Tim Major.

INTRODUCTION

With new crime TV series hitting our screens every week, and new authors appearing on the scene almost as frequently, the modern obsession with all things criminal shows no sign of abating. As mystery fiction becomes more readily available in translation, readers are also finding new hidey-holes within the worlds of Scandi noir, or Japanese *honkaku* and *shin-honkaku*. Crime writers aren't inclined to rest on their laurels, either – they're forever devising new puzzles and mysteries for readers to unravel, and fiendishly immoral murderers to pique our fascination. All driven by that one haunting phrase:

There's been a murder...

THE MEANS

What is crime fiction?

Despite the genre existing in the glare of near ubiquity and the oft-repeated analysis of its tropes, structures and techniques, there remains something oddly elusive about crime fiction. A mystery novel may be a puzzle comprised of interlocking pieces which can be held at arm's length for inspection with a logician's eye, but behind the dazzle of the design lies the eternal murk of humankind: death, evil, guilt and murder. These are the stuff of crime fiction.

The following essays present three points of entry for an author's deeper exploration of this terrain. Is it the puzzle of the well-crafted mystery that draws you in, a simple question that became a genre in its own right: whodunit? Or are you drawn to the darker side of human nature, and the base impulses that drive a person to break not only the laws of the land, but the unwritten rules of humanity?

It Bleeds

Tess Little

You are invited to open a door. Behind this door, you are told, you will find a room, and within this room you will find a question. Everything you need to answer this question sits within this room.

You push open the door. Behind it lies the room you wanted to find. The library nook of a gentleman's study, with a crackling fire and leather Chesterfield and the sweet scent of wood-shelved volumes. Or, no: a metal table and chair, white walls with a mirror, several feet wide, affixed at exactly eye level. Or, no: the rush and jolt of a train passing fields at dusk – warm in the carriage but cold from the window, no other passengers in sight.

Whatever room it is you desire, whatever room you find yourself in, you will find within it three things:

A folded square of paper;

A cardboard box, just big enough to fit an orange;

On the floor, blood, dark and terrible.

You tear your eyes from this puddle, pull yourself back to the task. You are here to find, and to answer, a question.

The paper seems the natural place to begin. Something solid, there. Gingerly avoiding the blood, you approach the arm of the leather sofa, the plain metal chair, or the train table upon which the note sits. You unfold it. Scratched in ink/scrawled in biro/hammered by a typewriter, it reads: *What is mystery?*

* * *

You lower yourself to the Chesterfield/metal chair/train seat and ponder this question. What is mystery?

You start with the words on the paper. That last word: *mystery*. The defining characteristic of any mystery novel or short story – or film, for that matter – must be the presence of a mystery. And what is a mystery? The answer might lie in the note, too: the punctuation. A mystery is a question. Something unexplained – for the writer to know and the reader to discover.

This fosters a certain feeling, which gnaws beneath your ribcage now. An unsettling, because you don't yet know where this is going, but excitement, too. You've nursed such a feeling before – when reading about a missing person in the news, when studying museum artefacts from the distant past, when looking at a shelf of dusty tomes, an unnaturally placed mirror, or passing unfamiliar landscape at night.

A question draws attention to the unknown, creates suspense, provokes curiosity. This is the nature of mystery.

Yet that can't be all there is to the genre, because every story contains mystery of some form. In a romance, the question is: will they, won't they? Reading horror, we wonder: who, or what, is creaking the floorboards? Sci-fi and fantasy often give rise to a whole cascade of mysteries: how does this technology work, how does this magic manifest, who will wield it, to what ends?

The unexplained sparks stories of all genres – when a stranger knocks on the door, say, or a peculiar object appears. The more you consider mystery, the more expansive it seems.

* * *

Perhaps mystery novels centre on questions of a more specific nature. Your eyes dart to the blood. Finally you acknowledge the dread in your stomach – the suspicion that something horrific has happened here. But what? A murder? An attack? Upon whom? By whom? And where is the body?

Whatever the answer, clearly a crime has occurred. Crimes make perfect mysteries, you think. The perpetrator, in concealing their identity, provides a neat question. Take Agatha Christie's *Murder on the Orient Express*: who killed the American businessman found stabbed in his train compartment, snow-stranded in Eastern Croatia?

And a compelling question, too. Not only because of the high stakes involved – justice, ensuring the culprit won't strike again – but also the sordid nature. When the fundamental rules of society are contravened – *thou shalt not kill, thou shalt not steal* – curiosity prickles. That enduring mystery: what would drive one man to end another?

You are still staring at the blood on the floor. Is it growing? No, a trick of the light.

You tilt your head this way and that, trying to discern how the body would have lain, picturing the weapon, but the shape is indistinct. The blood has pooled and puddled over time, seeping into the Persian rug/the concrete floor/the plain patterned carpet of the carriage.

You realise crimes make compelling questions not because they *must* be answered, with everything at stake, but also because they *can* be answered – because, like riddles, they have solutions. The snowdrift outside Christie's Orient Express is pristine, so the killer must have been another passenger. The criminal is there, to be rooted out. The answer is waiting to be found.

And while the culprit may have tried to conceal the evidence, something will always remain. Crimes alter the fabric of the world: one less person walking, talking, breathing; an object missing, or discovered somewhere it shouldn't be; the room, rearranged; a guilty conscience. Threads to follow. One question will lead to another, one small mystery to the next: if Christie tells us that a handkerchief embroidered with the letter 'H' is found in her American businessman's train compartment, might that have belonged to the killer? Who, on the Orient Express, has a name beginning with that letter?

Or the clues might lie in suspects' backgrounds. Often the true mystery is the question of the characters' relationships. Find out who Christie's passengers are, work out who the businessman was to them, and you'll know why he met his death on that snow-stalled train.

* * *

For these reasons, you decide upon detective fiction as your clearest example of mystery: a story not only sparked by, but continually propelled by, questions. But as you test your hypothesis, you grow less confident that the presence of a crime is the defining characteristic of the genre at large.

Golden Age author Josephine Tey is widely considered one of the greatest mystery writers, yet her novel *The Franchise Affair* follows attempts to prove no crime happened at all – that Marion Sharpe and her mother were falsely accused of kidnapping, imprisoning and abusing local schoolgirl Betty Kane. (The mystery here becomes: if the Sharpes have never laid eyes on Kane, as they claim, then how does Kane remember the interior of their house in detail? Why would she frame two women she'd never met?)

In *Gaudy Night* by Dorothy L. Sayers, another master, the initial mystery comes in the form of a vicious note – unpleasant, but not quite criminal. Maria Semple's *Where'd You Go, Bernadette* follows a fifteen-year-old's attempts to track down her missing mother – a disappearance precipitated not by murder or theft, but neighbourly disputes, and no less intriguing for this. Considering examples such as these, you eliminate the possibility that mystery is a subgenre of crime.

Nor is the inverse true – there are countless crime novels which don't centre on the investigation of a crime in its aftermath, but instead describe its unfolding. *A Helping Hand* by Celia Dale, for example, opens as former nurse Maisie Evans and her husband holiday in Italy following the death of their elderly lodger, Aunt Flo. While abroad, they meet widow

Cynthia Fingal and her niece Lena, who resents the burden of caring for her aunt. The Evans couple offers to take in Mrs Fingal, care for her as they did for Flo. But the reader already suspects, and soon learns, that ulterior motives lie beneath this offer: the care will take a sinister turn. The suspense Dale weaves, then, is not mystery's intrigue. Rather, a creeping unease, as the reader awaits the inevitable.

Then there are those novels exploring underworlds – stories that, even where they contain mysteries here and there, are primarily fuelled by attempts to best rivals and law enforcement. In Graham Greene's *Brighton Rock* and J.J. Connolly's *Layer Cake*, the veil is not lifted inch by inch, but thrown off from the very first page. Gangs! Mobs! Murder! Torture! Guns! Knives! Drugs! Money! Sex! Betrayal! Good versus Evil! And danger, everywhere.

* * *

The blood is still soaking into the floor, and you still have your question. What is mystery? Not the investigation of a crime, necessarily, but the investigation of a question—

Wait, yes, perhaps that's it. Mystery centres not on the unknown but its gradual elimination: deducing, deciphering, detection. This would explain why certain crime novels take the form of mysteries while others do not.

Your thoughts return to that clear example of mystery: detective fiction. Perhaps there's something, here, of the wider genre's essence – a subgenre which distils, even codifies, certain conventions of the genre at large.

Author Ronald Knox explored these conventions in his introduction to *The Best English Detective Stories of 1928*. His definition of detective fiction is straightforward:

> A detective story must have as its main interest the unravelling of a mystery; a mystery whose elements are clearly presented to the reader at an early stage in the proceedings, and whose nature is such as to arouse curiosity, a curiosity which is gratified at the end.

This was followed by a Decalogue in which Knox (also, notably, a Catholic priest) set down the subgenre's Ten Commandments. No supernatural explanations were permitted, nor unannounced identical twins, no culpable detectives – and certainly no *deus ex machina* events. If the author contravened these rules, they weren't giving the reader a fair chance to deduce the mystery for themselves.

Of course not, you think. It would spoil the game, cheating the reader. Because a detective novel *is* a game, or more specifically, a kind of puzzle.

You are irritated with yourself for not considering this sooner – you're certain you've heard it said before.

But now this realisation (or recollection) sets your thoughts skittering on. A puzzle is a game, and what do games do? They create closed arenas, limiting actions with rules and objectives, asking players to devote themselves to particular tasks. If detective novels are puzzles, then their closed arenas are the confines of story.

Not all mystery novels are puzzles – they needn't necessarily adhere to Knox's rules. But it still holds that they have as their main interest 'the unravelling of a mystery', and that this mystery arises from, and is contained by, story. In *Six Walks in the Fictional Woods*, Umberto Eco (a writer of mystery himself, of course, as well as philosopher and critic) describes fictional worlds as 'small worlds'. By bracketing the human experience, he says, novels enclose the reader in a 'finite' world, thus leading them 'to explore it in depth', and, 'one way or another, to take it seriously'.

Here is the question, says the mystery author. Here are the characters, their setting, the clues they leave behind – and the answer to the question, the gratification of your curiosity, lies somewhere in this small world.

No *deus ex machina*, indeed. Each detective novel its own locked room.

* * *

You glance at the door through which you entered this library/interrogation room/train carriage – wonder, briefly, whether it locked behind you.

Over the years you've read various locked-room mysteries: stories where a crime occurs in a space near-hermetically sealed, door locked from the inside only, and yet the perpetrator is nowhere to be found. A puzzle within the puzzle: not who committed the crime, but *how*?

The 'impossible murder' is, the unnamed narrator of Seishi Yokomizo's *The Honjin Murders* states, 'a genre that any self-respecting detective novelist will attempt at some point'. They add, 'Constructing a solution is an appealing challenge to the author' – as though the ultimate riddle is not for the reader (in solving any locked-room novel's particular crime), but the author (in solving the archetypal problem in their own ingenuous way, mathematicians devising new proofs).

Yokomizo's offering centres on a newlywed couple found 'slashed and soaked in blood' on their wedding night. The groom is the eldest son of the Ichiyanagi family, who have 'distinguished ancestry'; his bride, the daughter of a lowly tenant farmer. The couple have retired to an annexe on the Ichiyanagi estate when the guests in the main house hear blood-curdling cries and the twangs of the koto, a string instrument, 'being plucked with wild abandon'. By the time they make it to the annexe, the killer is nowhere to be found. All the rain shutters are locked, there are no openings large enough to climb in or out, no footsteps in the surrounding snow – only a katana 'stuck blade-first' about six feet away.

The Honjin Murders makes abundantly clear that this is a puzzle. At one point, a diagram of the annexe is provided, annotated with numbers that correspond to evidence found through the novel, right down to 'pile of fallen leaves'. The characters themselves even refer to the scene as 'the puzzle of this murder' and a 'locked room mystery'.

They would know: private detective Kosuke Kindaichi, drafted in to help police, passes idle moments reading mystery novels, and one of the suspects, the youngest Ichiyanagi son, is an 'avid' reader too. Kosuke almost falls over with amazement when he happens upon a bookcase crammed with 'every book of mystery or detective fiction ever published in Japan, both domestic and foreign' – Arthur Conan Doyle, Maurice Leblanc, Japanese writers all the way from Ruiko Kuriowa to Mushitaro Oguri – and 'the original, untranslated works of Ellery Queen, Dickson Carr, Freeman Wills Crofts and Agatha Christie, etc. etc. etc.' Did the killer learn from these masters?

* * *

Like other twentieth-century Japanese murder mysteries, *The Honjin Murders* explicitly grapples with the conventions of the subgenre. Another such novel, *The Decagon House Murders*, by Yukito Ayatsuji, begins with the characters discussing the trope of the 'chalet in a snowstorm' (used by mystery authors to create 'a sealed environment') just as they are heading straight for one themselves.

They're students, members of their university's mystery club, each nicknamed for a mystery author: Poe, Agatha, Carr, Orczy, Leroux, Ellery. A fisherman is ferrying them to an uninhabited island – the site of a fire, only six months before, which burned down a mansion. Four bodies were found in the wreckage. Keen to investigate, the students set up camp in the only building on the island still standing: the Decagon House. Until, that is, an unknown killer picks them off, one by one.

This comes as no surprise to the reader, who has, even before the first death, encountered multiple references to Christie's *And Then There Were None* – the template for any tale in which a murder occurs in an isolated location, and then another murder, and another, with the frantic tension mounting as everyone tries to find the killer before they become the next victim.

Christie's novel is one of the bestselling books of all time – the plot has inspired so many screen and page reworkings, it virtually forms its own trope. The same could be said of two other Christie novels, whose titles are now shorthand for certain mystery solutions: *The Murder of Roger Ackroyd* and *Murder on the Orient Express*. Detective fiction is a genre rich in tropes and self-reference. Just as chess players deploy openings and variations devised by the players before them, so are there established ways to play the game of writing mystery.

In the opening of *The Decagon House Murders*, student Ellery asserts that, in his opinion:

> mystery fiction is, at its core, a kind of intellectual puzzle. An exciting game of reasoning in the form of a novel. A game between the reader and the great detective, or the reader and the author. Nothing more or less than that.

Then, in a diatribe against 'gritty social realism', he lists everything he looks for in such fiction:

> What mystery novels need are – some might call me old-fashioned – a great detective, a mansion, a shady cast of residents, bloody murders, impossible crimes and never-before-seen tricks played by the murderer.

Your definition of mystery is more expansive than this hard-line detective fan's, but you admit that when you first unfolded your note, this was the kind of mystery that leapt to mind. Those building blocks: a mysterious setting; a closed circle; a sinister act; a shrewd detective.

* * *

Maybe this is what mystery is – or any genre, for that matter: a collection of tropes. A body of ideas which the writer can draw upon for inspiration. And as the tradition takes shape, so too does it shape the reader, their expectations. A reader will expect to encounter different settings, characters, maybe even different registers of language or plot points depending on whether they have lifted off the shelves a courtroom thriller, a police procedural, hardboiled, noir, or true crime.

More broadly, any novel centring on a mystery will come with expectations too. That feeling of curiosity, intrigue, suspense you identified earlier – this is key, and mystery tropes foster and prolong this feeling. The foreshadowing, the clues, the red herrings, the twists.

Do tropes define genre, or does genre engender tropes? The answer could be either, or both at once. Either way, you know tropes aren't prescriptive: mystery writers will take some, leave others, and all manner of writers can draw upon the mystery tradition – adopting its page-turning, rug-pulling techniques without plunging in headfirst.

Any story can take the form of an investigation, with the

discovery of clues, the testing of hypotheses (see A.S. Byatt, *Possession*). Any story can feature misinterpretations that mislead both protagonist and reader (as in Ian McEwan's *Atonement*). Novels structured around a character slowly revealing their past, bringing the reader to the present day, introduce natural mystery (Mohsin Hamid, *The Reluctant Fundamentalist*), as do certain characters, certain settings. Anita Brookner's *Hotel du Lac* takes place in the titular hotel, out of season, introducing the protagonist, Edith, to a cast of idiosyncratic characters who would fit right into a Christie. The mystery, here, is Edith herself, nursing a wound that is hinted to the reader from the opening pages. Secrets are always mysterious.

When you first entered this library/interrogation room/ carriage, you decided that stories of all genres centred on mysteries of one kind or another. Now you see that the mystery novel's form – its conceits, devices, tropes – has its own wide reach as well. Mystery is a genre which bleeds into the rest.

Yes – your gaze returns to the bloodstain – it bleeds.

* * *

You feel more hopeless than ever now: if mystery isn't distinct, how can you answer your question?

Yet a detective can still deduce something about a missing corpse from the traces it left behind. If mystery is a body of ideas, bleeding out, that seeping is evidence too.

You crouch on the rug/concrete/carpet. At the very edges of the stain, the crimson has thinned, blending with the ornate swirls of the rug/colouring the grey/tingeing the carpet pattern. Perhaps boundary cases can help you in your task: what is it that blends and bleeds?

When you think of mystery beyond crime, the first works that come to mind are those of Daphne du Maurier. Gothic mysteries: novels set in dark, isolated reaches (a romantic country estate, a gloomy coaching inn) where some secret festers in the shadows. Du Maurier stories are often propelled by the protagonist's attempts to uncover such secrets: did cousin Rachel poison Ambrose Ashley? Why is Maxim so haunted by his dead wife, Rebecca? How does the Jamaica Inn survive with no guests? Beyond du Maurier there are more examples, yet. In Shirley Jackson's *We Have Always Lived in the Castle*, the Blackwood family's tragedy is revealed little by little. Mystery and the gothic are ideal bedfellows. What hides in the shadows, indeed.

Then there are fantasy-mysteries, in which worldbuilding either gives rise to mystery or constitutes the mystery itself. As in, for example, Susanna Clarke's *Piranesi*, which casts both the titular protagonist and the reader adrift in the mystical, cryptic 'House': a world of great halls and vestibules, 'hundreds upon hundreds' of marble statutes, and crashing tides of seawater which rush up the stone staircases 'making all the Statues tremble'.

The same is true of sci-fi-mystery. Take China Miéville's *The City and the City*, in which there is both a traditional mystery driving protagonist Inspector Tyador Borlú (who killed the unnamed young woman and dumped her body between a 'derelict tower' and a skatepark?) and also a fundamental mystery for the reader: how can two cities separated by an insurmountable border exist in the exact same location? As the novel unfolds, so the two questions entangle. Science fiction, fantasy and horror provide fertile ground for mystery, and vice versa: each genre draws upon its own tradition of the unknown.

Comparing these works to detective fiction, you find they are less formulaic, yes, perhaps not puzzles, but they still follow Knox's opening maxim: they have as their 'main interest the unravelling of a mystery'. Crucially, 'unravelling' is as central as the mystery itself. A mystery novel, or a hybrid mystery, is not simply sparked by a question – the characters, the story are propelled by its unravelling too.

* * *

Your knees are aching; they crack as you stand. Of course, what many hybrid cases lack is the presence of a detective. This doesn't trouble you – you've never felt detectives were a defining feature of mystery so much as detective fiction – but you wonder: what role do such characters play in the unravelling?

Within the story, they lead the investigation, finding clues, forming theories, making the fateful accusation. For the reader they are something more. Not an avatar, not quite a rival, nor a colleague, a guide, but some mixture of all these elements. A go-between, almost, bridging author (with their omniscient grasp of the mystery's solution) and reader (with all their initial ignorance). The detective will feed the reader facts, observations, hypotheses, but a good detective will hypothesise one step behind, giving the reader a chance to work it out for themselves.

You've heard it said that detective fiction is unique in its ability to draw in the reader, how it embroils them in joining the dots. But this doesn't feel quite right. All works of literature ask the reader to interpret. A sentence as a string of clues: put the words together, the author says, and *you* tell *me* what I mean. It isn't simply that – as you mused when you first entered this room – the author has all the knowledge and the reader all the ignorance, it's that the reader is asked to understand the author's intentions. 'To read a book well,' Virginia Woolf once argued, 'one should read it as if one were writing it. Begin not by sitting on the bench among the judges but by standing in the dock with the criminal.'

Mystery brings this relationship to the fore. Nothing exemplifies this better than a successful twist, which emerges from the author's knowledge, the reader's attempts to work out what the author knows, and then the author's subversion of those attempts.

Every mystery should include at least one twist, you decide. A readily guessable mystery is no mystery at all. Twists are fundamental to the atmosphere, with the reader's delight lying as much in anticipation of trickery as in the trick itself. Like a child winding a jack-in-the-box, ready to spring at any moment.

* * *

You've been haunted by such a feeling since you first entered this room. You glance at the corners, as though someone might be hiding there. In doing so, your vision skirts the cardboard box. How could you have forgotten the box?

You sit at the walnut/metal/train table, take the box into your hands. It's no jack-in-the-box, but you hear a rattle – there's something inside. Perhaps this object is meant to exemplify the point you were considering: the author's knowledge, their ability to wrong-foot the reader. If so, you'll give it a shot – you'll play the guessing game.

You shake the box again, feel the shifting weight. Only slightly, though – it's something small. And useful, you hope. Like a pencil – you could stand to make some notes.

Or maybe it's another clue. Galvanised by this hope, you hurry to open the box.

There is nothing inside. What made the noise? You shake the box again, hoping something might fall out, and as you do, you find the cardboard itself is weighty – the inner flap of the lid was simply knocking against the inside.

Ah, you think. But this is what a twist should be: constructed from the thing itself. Infuriating, inescapable. You had no firm beliefs about what the box would contain beyond the belief that it contained something. You should have known, therefore, it would contain nothing at all. You laugh at yourself.

Didn't this guessing game show something of your own expectations? Your hopes for a clue? This is what a twist does, revealing not only the truth of the mystery: it reveals the reader to themselves.

* * *

It's an oft-repeated maxim (sometimes attributed to Aristotle, sometimes to Flannery O'Connor) that the ending of a story should be 'surprising yet inevitable'. This matters more, you think, for mysteries than any other genre.

But how difficult the challenge of truly surprising readers who expect – no, demand – to be surprised.

Knox ended his Decalogue with a lamentation:

> Nobody can have failed to notice that while the public demand for mystery stories remains unshaken, the faculty for writing a good mystery story is rare, and the means of writing one with any symptom of originality about it becomes rarer with each succeeding year. The game is getting played out; before long, it is to be feared, all the possible combinations will have been used up.

Writers have continued to produce mysteries both original and brilliant in the century since Knox wrote those words – but perhaps he was correct as far as conventional detective fiction goes. True experimentation is more readily found in those areas where the genre has bled and blurred.

Or, indeed, where authors have subverted expectations altogether, in mysteries metafictional, postmodern, experimental – you still remember the jolt you felt seven pages into Paul Auster's *City of Glass*, when the protagonist, Quinn, answers a ringing phone and the voice asks to speak to 'Paul Auster.

Of the Auster Detective Agency'. 'There's nothing I can do for you,' Quinn replies. 'There is no Paul Auster here.'

As much as you loved them, as much as detective fiction is ripe for metafiction, those postmodern mysteries still irritate. You still remember that impulse which seized you with the last sentence: to reach through the pages and shake the author and ask what the hell they thought they were doing. What is it that unnerved? The frustration of your conviction that a mystery novel will, should, must feed an answer. *The Magus* by John Fowles, *Death in Her Hands* by Ottessa Moshfegh – these are novels which upend convention, leaving the reader with the unease mystery fosters, expanding beyond the confines of their covers, because no solution is provided. Life, after all, is a mystery with no clear answer.

The note, with its question, is in your pocket. You fiddle with the paper, flick it with your thumb.

Postmodern and/or experimental mysteries are, then, exceptions that prove the rule: a mystery novel cannot simply *present* a reader with a question, does not simply revolve around *attempts to find* an answer; there must always *be* an answer too. If, as Knox wrote, the nature of detective fiction was both 'to arouse curiosity' and to gratify that curiosity 'at the end', the same holds for mystery at large.

This is, you feel, the final piece of your puzzle. Mystery, as a genre, is defined by three things. First, the question. Then, the act of deduction. And last, an answer. And all within the confines of the novel's 'small world', which is to say: character, place, and plot.

This definition encapsulates your paradigmatic example of detective fiction, but also gothic mysteries, sci-fi mysteries, fantasy mysteries, espionage mysteries – any story in which both protagonist and reader are driven to reveal the truth, uncover the hidden. And as the protagonist arrives at an answer, so too does the reader – if they haven't worked it out already, that is – bringing the story to its close.

* * *

You wander to the blazing fire/your own reflection/the misting window. Your hypothesis feels right, but you can't quite tell how it relates to this room. As though the true puzzle was not your question but the strange situation – the invitation, the door; the note, blood, box.

Those objects still unsettle you. All three sent your thoughts in the right direction but you have no clearer notion of their origins. Where did the blood come from? Who left this box? Where's the author of the note?

Rest assured, these are not real mysteries. You know the culprit. It was me, the author of this essay (didn't Woolf tell you writers are criminal?). I conjured these fictional props, this little mystery, from the words on these pages. It was a ploy, yes, but that's not to say the props had no purpose at all. My point was not to provide you with clues revealing specific facts, but to, quite simply, provide you with clues.

You strike your hand against the table. Of course! The answer was there all along. Not in the particular clues but in the fact of their presence. *Their presence in this fictional room.* The true puzzle, you see, was the situation, and the situation was the mystery – the closed world you entered when you pushed open the door, when you read the first lines of this essay:

> You are invited to open a book. Within its pages, you are told, you will find a story and within this story you will find a question. Everything you need to answer this question sits within this story.

This is the nature of mystery, as a genre – what it promises the reader, what it invites them to do. The task was always the answer.

The fire pops/the fluorescent light bulb flickers/the train horn blares, as though in confirmation. Now the question has been answered, you may leave. And perhaps the leather Chesterfield/the bare walls/the view from the train window, entice you to linger a while longer – if only to delay your return to reality. Then again, there are other doors, other books to open. Other rooms, other worlds, other questions to answer. Other stories to read and to write.

The Killer Inside Me: Writing the Criminal

Charlie Higson

I've always enjoyed crime fiction. As a teenager I started on the American classics, Raymond Chandler, Dashiell Hammett and James M. Cain, and then, when I hit my twenties, in the 1980s, there was an explosion of American crime writing – authors like Elmore Leonard, James Ellroy and George V. Higgins were coming into their own, but there was also a renewed interest in classic pulp fiction, rebranded as 'American Noir'.

Forgotten classics from the 1940s through to the '70s were being rediscovered and, crucially, reprinted, by publishers (the two key ones being Black Box and Black Lizard). Most of these stories had originally appeared in pulp magazines or as dirt cheap 'dime store' paperbacks. The pulp magazines (so called because they were printed on the lowest quality paper) didn't only publish crime fiction, there was true crime, westerns, romances, sci-fi, adventure stories and lurid tales of teenage drug taking, lesbianism and delinquency.

The cheap, mass-produced paperbacks had the same aesthetic. They were designed to stand out on the shelves of drug stores and gas stations. They had unsubtle covers, usually depicting large-breasted, scantily-clad women, going head-to-head with mean-looking men with hard jaws and greased-back hair. It was a world of guns, bourbon and cigarette smoke – lipstick, stockings, cars, motels… with strap lines like: 'She was a hell of a woman, and that's where he was headed.' This was clearly outsider fiction, about men and women living on the fringes of society, transgressors who could be relied on to behave badly. Stories about lawbreakers rather than lawmen. And if there were any policemen or detectives in these books, they could be relied on to behave as badly as everyone else.

But these weren't just titillating tales calculated to arouse people's basest instincts. As long as the stories delivered all the elements promised on the covers – plenty of sex and violence – the readers were happy, and this gave the 'pulp' authors the freedom to write about whatever they wanted. As long as somebody got laid and somebody got murdered and somebody got beaten to a bloody mess, the writers could be as inventive, experimental and creative as any respected 'literary' novelist. The big difference being that these books were disposable, designed to be read quickly rather than discussed by pipe-smoking academics.

My love of these books inspired me to explore the crime genre more widely. I became obsessed with books that dealt with the darker side of humanity. I was able to easily get hold of works by 'pulp' authors like Charles Willeford, David Goodis and Cornell Woolrich and make many other delighted discoveries. Dorothy B. Hughes, who wrote the amazing early 'serial killer' novel from 1947, *In a Lonely Place*, the great Patricia Highsmith, Margaret Millar. And it wasn't just America noir I was interested in, some great English writers too – Derek Raymond, Ted Lewis (who wrote the novel that *Get Carter* is based on), Patrick Hamilton (from whom we get the concept of 'gaslighting').

So it was that I felt I had a reasonably good overview of crime fiction and had read quite widely. Why then was it that when asked in interviews, or in Q&As at crime writing festivals, whether I'd read such-and-such a bestselling crime writer, did I come up blank? Why had I not read any of the hugely popular modern crime authors? It was only when I was asked to write a similar piece to this that I figured it out.

I love crime fiction.

But I love crime fiction about criminals, rather than people solving crimes.

Looking back at the triumvirate I read as a teenager – Chandler, Hammet and Cain – I see now that they run the full gamut of crime fiction. At one end is Philip Marlowe, the archetype of the incorruptible crime fighter. In the middle are the much more compromised protagonists of Hammet's criminal universe. The detective in his classic *Red Harvest*, known only as 'The Continental Op', is a much shadier figure, straddling the worlds of crime and the law, comfortable being on either side of the line, as he plays warring gangs off against each other. One of the 'gangs' being a corrupt police force.

James M. Cain's protagonists are at the other end of the spectrum to Marlowe. They are for the most part law-breakers – murderers, adulterers, men who've fallen on hard times and turn to petty crime.

And that's the end of the spectrum I'm drawn to.

This is why I prefer Barbara Vine's psychological thrillers to the police procedurals about Inspector Wexford written by her alter ego, Ruth Rendell. Don't get me wrong. I don't hate detective fiction. I moved on from the American classics to the likes of Agatha Christie, Joseph Wambaugh, Ed McBain, Robert B. Parker, Ross MacDonald, Mark Billingham, Jo Ide and Michael Connelly, and have always found much to enjoy in these books. But, in the end, police procedurals and detective stories don't give me the hit I crave from crime fiction. (I have to confess I find the popularity of Sherlock Holmes mystifying, and always think I must be missing something.)

I want to see the underside of things – the dark side. Not from a detective's point of view, briefly shining their torch at the ugly, crawling life beneath the rock before moving on. I want to see it from the point of view of the slugs and the worms and the woodlice.

I don't want to be reassured; I want to be unnerved. So, forgive me if most of my references (apart from TV and film) are very much last century. I guess I'm very much last century myself. Maybe I'm wrong, but not many novelists today are writing the type of crime fiction I enjoy. My frustration with detection-based crime fiction is two-fold – and I am making some gross oversimplifications here:

1. Crimes are presented as puzzles – mysteries to be unravelled. We follow detectives who follow the clues and eventually expose the villains. In the process, we learn very little about why the criminals do what they do. If you're always trying to hide your culprit, then, beyond a pat explanation, we'll never really know why they were driven to murder.
2. Detection stories present us with the comforting myth that crimes can all be solved, that everything will be made right and order will be restored. They are basic good-versus-evil tales. Light versus dark. Torch versus slug. And I'm not sure the world works that way.

So, this piece is about what lies underneath. It's about the people who commit the crimes, not the people who solve them. It's about the men and women who appeared on the covers of those dime store paperbacks, who I find more compelling than all those police and detectives, no matter how much they're given 'character' by having a love of jazz, or chess, or classic cars, or Italian cooking. In the end, they all tend to be the same person and share the same characteristics. They're loners. They have problems with authority and so are always slightly on the outside. They won't do what they're told. They find it difficult to hold together any kind of relationship. Largely because the job is always more important to them than anything else in their lives. They throw themselves into their work in order to not have to confront their own problems. And they're driven to shine a light in the darkness, to catch the criminal, to put right the wrongs of the world.

Which, nine times out of ten, they do. They save the victim in peril, even if they can't save themselves.

Raymond Chandler famously summed this character up – 'down these mean streets a man must go who is not himself mean, who is neither tarnished nor afraid'.

It's a beautiful archetype, tapping into all our heroic myths and legends – Sir Gawain and Parsifal, Roland of Roncesvalles, Robin Hood. But anyone who's followed the recent scandals within the Metropolitan Police in the UK, or the depressingly regular exposure of miscarriages of justice, will know that this image of the policeman as knight in shining armour is some way from reality. Endless fly-on-the-wall police documentaries also show the daily, dull plod-work of an actual police force. No glamorous murder walls and 'Aha' moments in interviews. No sudden deciphering of a cryptic message. It's mostly cross-referencing on computers, boring checking of forensic evidence and witness statements and hours spent scouring through CCTV footage.

I've always felt we could learn more about the world by studying criminals rather than detectives. And nobody wrote about the criminal mind better than Jim Thompson. It was inevitable, back in my twenties, that I would eventually make my way to Jim Thompson. The King of the Pulps. And when I first read one of his books I was stopped in my tracks. It was clear that Thompson was something different. He took things to a different level. He was some kind of twisted genius. He really seemed to understand the cross-wired thought processes that can lead someone to commit violence, betrayal and murder. He repeatedly shows us the self-justification and self-delusion of a killer as they try to convince us – and themselves – that they're doing the right thing. They're absolutely sure that we'll understand why they have to do what they're going to do, and that we'll agree with them that it's the only thing that can be done. And then we can then only stand back and watch in appalled horror as they proceed to do some of the most terrible things imaginable.

Thompson's books read fast and they were often written fast. If he ran out of money, he'd hammer out another book. He often wrote to order, in a burst of creative energy and often with a lack of scrutiny, and his writing was usually fuelled by booze. As a result, the quality can be variable. At the top end are classics like *The Killer Inside Me*, *Pop 1280*, *Savage Night*, *The Grifters*, *A Hell of a Woman* and *The Getaway*. At the other end of the scale are lesser works where the writing can sometimes feel like the weird ramblings of a drunk who's been up all night, railing at the world, full of self-pity and self-disgust. The books are never less than compelling, however, and there's always at least one passage that brings you up short, when one of his characters has a dying revelation, or a frightening insight, or slips into a chaotic world of madness in which we can never be sure whether the events being described are in the character's head or are really happening.

My favourite is a nightmarish – and yet disturbingly funny – sequence in *Savage Night*, in which our hero, the gangland killer Little Charlie Bigger, holes up on a farm where the owner claims to be harvesting assholes.

Thompson had a rootless, dysfunctional and disjoined early life. He was a teenage alcoholic who got involved in far-left politics in the 1930s, and took various dead-end jobs – in an aircraft factory, on the desk of a seedy hotel, as a roustabout in the Texas oil fields – and mixed with the sort of damaged characters he wrote about. His books are rooted in a gritty, sweaty, cloying, claustrophobic reality that always seems to fall apart and tip over into chaos and often oblivion – like the inevitable end to a night of heavy drinking.

His characters are mostly small-time misfits, grifters, sociopaths, losers who have nevertheless made some begrudging headway in the world by working outside the conventional norms of civilised society. They live by their own rules and often end up completely falling through the net of civilisation.

Thompson's books show us the world from the criminals' point of view – from the other side of the fence. And the conclusions they come to are very different to the standard police/detective story. They're about as far from 'cosy crime' as you can get. By the end of each story, nothing has been put right, everything is broken, and we've somehow wound up in hell. In the case of the desperate bank robbers on the run in *The Getaway* (1958), literally so, as they get away to the terrifying criminal kingdom of El Rey in Mexico, from which there is no escape. The last chapters of this book are devastating and like nothing else in crime fiction.

It's interesting that out of all the forgotten American crime writers rediscovered in the 1980s, Thompson is just about the only one still in print today. Luckily, though, his writing is strong enough to balance out all those reassuring police detectives single-handedly.

Policemen *do* feature as central characters in some of Thompson's books, but they're corrupt and violent and often the biggest criminals in town. Chandler's ideal for a detective was someone who wasn't mean, tarnished nor afraid. Thompson's characters are all of those things. And more. His policemen don't heal the wounds of a damaged society, they don't right the wrongs of bad men, because *they are* the bad men, they themselves are the killers.

Nick Corey, for instance, sheriff of the fly speck on the map that is Pottsville, Texas – Population 1280 – as well as being mean, tarnished and afraid, is also lazy, self-serving and self-pitying. He does no crime solving. He arrests no one. He's only sheriff because he can be relied on to do precisely nothing and let people get on with their lives. He's a useful idiot. Or so people think. As it turns out, Nick finds it easier to simply kill anyone he doesn't like.

Thompson shows us a disconcerting world in which the people who are supposed to be holding everything together and protecting us are doing the opposite. Recent history has shown us that it's entirely plausible that the man stalking the young woman, before sexually assaulting and murdering her, is a police officer. That idea makes us all uncomfortable. And Thompson's books – obsessed, as they are, with transgression – can sometimes be an uncomfortable read. We are taken into the minds of some very damaged characters and invited to share their thoughts.

Another lawman, Lou Ford, the protagonist of *The Killer Inside Me* (1952), is the most awful and the most notorious. He's a genial, but deadly-dull, deputy sheriff who sadistically spouts cliches and greetings card platitudes in an attempt to bore people to death and hide his true nature as a very damaged, controlling, misogynistic sadist. As an out-and-out psychopath, Lou is utterly plausible and utterly appalling. The scenes of his brutality are extremely hard to stomach. He inhabits a cynical, nihilistic, self-destructive world in which he hates everything and everyone – himself most of all. But if you want to try to understand how abusive relationships function, then this book will show you.

Compared to *The Killer Inside Me*, *Pop 1280* reads almost like a light-hearted comedy version of the same story – despite still having some very uncomfortable passages. And it's Thompson's use of jet-black humour that makes his books so startlingly unnerving. We can't help but laugh at Lou Ford's corny jokes and Nick Corey's misanthropic, self-justifying observations of the world. Which lead him to conclude that if everyone else is a shit, it'd be foolish not to be one yourself.

If we take Agatha Christie as the template for a standard detective story (and I don't think the conventions have significantly changed since her day), then we usually only really see the story from the point of view of the detective/investigator. The job of the mystery writer is to keep the identity of the 'murderer' (it's nearly always a murderer) secret until the end of the book. And it's the job of the murderer to keep their true nature hidden. We are taken through a series of twists, revelations, red herrings and dead ends before the big reveal. And the murder then only has a couple of pages at most to explain/justify what they did. This is all great fun, and very satisfying, but there can be no real psychological insight or depth because there just isn't time. Usually, we learn very little about the murderer, and their motives have to be clear, simple and simplistic.

They needed the money.

They resented something their victim had done to them in the past.

They were trying to cover up their own wrongdoing and get rid of a witness.

And so on.

In many of Thompson's books, his characters behave like Christie suspects, hiding their true nature from the world. Pretending to be what they're not. Conning society. But as we're seeing the story though their eyes, we learn a great deal about them, what their true nature is, and why they do what they do. Which, for me, is considerably more interesting and satisfying.

Most of Thompson's characters are variations of a 'con man'. A common psychopathic trait. They deceive others in order to control them.

Sherriff Nick Corey doesn't want anyone in his small town to know how corrupt he is, and that he's sleeping with several different women. So, he pretends to be a fool – harmless, stupid and untutored. But we know he's not, and he occasionally lets others see a glimpse of his clever, deceiving mind, in order to terrify them into doing what he wants.

Lou Ford uses his stultifying, homespun philosophising as a way to keep anyone from asking too many questions about him – they're too bored to even think about him.

Doc McCoy in *The Getaway* is, on the outside, a perfect, charming, Southern gentleman, with disarming manners, but we know him to be a pitiless psychopath, who will use and discard anybody to get what he wants. Including the woman who loves him.

Roy Dillon in *The Grifters* (1963) is perhaps the purest example of this type, as he's literally a con artist – a grifter.

The classic noir story shows the protagonist as a loser on a downward spiral. Everything they do to try to slow their descent only make things worse. Thompson's books don't end with the hero winning, the detective solving the crime, the bad guys rounded up, order restored, justice done, the world put to rights. The endings are usually a blow to the gut, just like the one given to Roy Dillon in *The Grifters*. He gets belly-punched in the first chapter and spends the rest of the book slowly dying from the damage to his insides.

His endings have a stench of the apocalypse about them. They're bleak and hopeless. And even as their worlds disintegrate around them, his characters refuse to accept they've done anything wrong.

You might ask, why write about these people in the first place? Well, for me, understanding *why* people commit crimes, and how they see the world, is more enlightening than following a clever sleuth piece a jigsaw puzzle together. But, beyond that, Thompson wrote about how he thought the world worked. His characters are convinced that they're merely doing what any person does. That humanity is rotten to the core. Everything that happens to his characters supports their pessimistic view of human nature and Thompson's argument is compellingly put. His most quoted line is 'Life is a bucket of shit with a barbed wire handle' (sorry, but I can't track down where it's from).

That attitude – and these books – aren't for everyone.

It's interesting that after the brief blossoming of outsider crime fiction in the 1980s, and an interest in books written from a criminal point of view, things veered in the opposite direction. There were a few British authors in the early 1990s that were inspired by American noir – Nicholas Blincoe, James Hawes and myself among them – but as the decade wore on crime shifted ever more into the mainstream, and towards detective fiction and police procedurals. Now, crime books regularly sit at the top of the bestseller charts. But it's a different kind of crime fiction to that which I enjoyed in my formative years.

I wrote four novels about psychopaths, murderers and criminals, with barely a policeman in sight. And, though the books performed respectably, I felt that I was out of step with the times. What the world wanted, and still does, is soap operas about the police. As I said before, Thompson aside, since the 1990s, few of the other outsider novelists have endured. It seems that if you want to sell a lot of crime books you need to come up with a new detective, with some charming quirks, who can appear in a long-running series, or an amateur sleuth who always gets to the bottom of things.

Or get into domestic noir. A thriving subgenre of crime writing that used to broadly fall into the category of psychological thrillers. The stories tend to be domestic dramas with either a twist or a mystery at their core to be unravelled. It seems to me that, because they revolve around the idea of secrets and lies and who can you trust, we're once again in the territory of the hidden killer.

To conclude, if you want to write about a convincing killer, you have to ask yourself – are you prepared to go there? Because, if you do, then down those mean streets *you* must walk. Not as a detective with a bright torch, but as a killer with a rusty knife.

All writers are actors. We create our characters and we act them out in our heads. I tend to go on long walks and run through dialogue between my characters, speaking out loud as I go. If you have earbuds in, people don't think you're mad, they just assume you're talking to someone on the phone. What I'm doing, though, is talking to my imaginary friends.

If you want to create a criminal, a sociopath, a person who does terrible things, are you prepared to spend time with them? To fully inhabit their personae? There must be a reason (perhaps a subject for a different essay and a different writer to unravel) why a crime writer leans towards either detectives or criminals.

The author Robert Cook, who wrote under the pen name Derek Raymond, is perhaps the British author who has the most doom-laden and degenerate smell of Jim Thompson about them. He was an upper-class drop-out who descended into a world of petty criminals, drug addicts, poets, revolutionaries, artists, musicians, prostitutes and outsiders in the 1960s and '70s, and eventually turned to crime writing. He wrote several books about a police department known as the Factory, a low-status unit who take on the all the unwanted, dead-end cases. A Slough House of the police world. His protagonist is an unnamed police officer in the familiar mould of the fictional detective – insubordinate, mouthy, drunken, pissed off and obsessed about putting right the pathetic wronged victims whose cases he has to solve.

We see a lot of the killers in Raymond's books. And we hear their inner voices. We also learn a lot about their victims, who our policemen strongly identifies with, and seems driven to become one of them himself. The books are upsetting, deliberately repulsive, depressing, funny, sadistic, masochistic and so dark that the central novels of the series – from *He Died With His Eyes Open* (1984) to *I Was Dora Suarez* (1990) – are known as the Black Books.

The Black Books become increasingly nasty, his killers ever more depraved, and his victims ever more extremely abused. I have a strong stomach and have taken most of what noir fiction can throw at me. But, like many others – including Cook's editor at the time – I found *I Was Dora Suarez* too revolting to finish.

Cook/Raymond said that writing the book broke him:

If you go down into the darkness, you must expect it to leave traces on you coming up – if you do come up… I wondered half way through Suarez if I would get through – I mean, if my reason would get through. For the trouble with an experience like Suarez is that you become what you're writing...

Jim Thompson was an alcoholic. The booze killed him when he was seventy, when none of his books were still in print.

Patricia Highsmith was described by J.G. Ballard as 'every bit as deviant and quirky as her mischievous heroes, and didn't seem to mind if everyone knew it'. Booze and fags did for her.

Ted Lewis (the creator of Jack Carter) died in 1982, aged forty-two, of alcohol-related causes.

Cancer did for Cook when he was sixty-three.

Happy writing.

The Deader the Better: On Writing the Murder

Andrew Gallix

Although ubiquitous in fiction, murder is mercifully rare in fact. The latest figures for England and Wales indicate that 11.7 murders per million population were perpetrated over a twelve-month period, that is fewer than 700 *in toto*. Most of us will go through life without ever witnessing or being affected by such a crime – let alone falling victim to it – and yet hardly a day goes by without encountering its gory spectacle on the screen or page. It is true that many violent films and novels originate in the United States, where the incidence of homicide is (for obvious reasons) far higher than in Europe, but this fact alone does not account for the yawning gap between the relative rarity of murder in real life and its relentless representation in works of the imagination. Some might say that these ever-recurring fictional killings are a kind of repetition compulsion through which our collective fear of meeting a gruesome death is tentatively exorcised. To which others might respond: no shit, Sherlock!

THE DEADER THE BETTER: ON WRITING THE MURDER

You will probably have noticed that crime in crime fiction is invariably murder, as Edgar Allan Poe advertised with his 'The Murders in the Rue Morgue' (1841), usually regarded as the first modern detective story. 'Burglaries/Muggings/Flesh Wounds in the Rue Morgue' simply would not have cut it. The sequel was pitched in similarly sensational style: 'The Murder of Marie Rogêt' (1842–43). At least ten Agatha Christie novels include 'Murder' in their titles, notably *The Murder of Roger Ackroyd* (1926) and *Murder on the Orient Express* (1934), while many others point most portentously to the spilling of blood ('Death', 'Body', etc.). In his oft-quoted 'Twenty Rules for Writing Detective Fiction' (*American Magazine*, 1928), S.S. Van Dine decrees that '[t]here simply must be a corpse in a detective novel, and the deader the corpse the better'. He goes on to argue that '[n]o lesser crime will suffice', presumably because murder is indeed the ultimate crime: a violation of the sanctity of life – the very principle underpinning human society. As such, it could be construed as a crime against humanity.

The perfunctory approach to murder in many classical whodunits may come, therefore, as something of a surprise. The act itself – seldom described in graphic detail – is frequently kept at arm's length by being expedited, or set in the (recent) past: in essence, the deed is done always-already. Thus sanitised, murder can serve its narrative purpose, which is to propel the investigation towards its teleological resolution. The mystery, it turns out, always has a rational explanation, the criminal is invariably brought to book; the reader gratified with a sense of closure and the victim all but forgotten – all's well that ends well. Murder in this context is almost incidental, the identity of the corpse being of little import, and yet it is also absolutely crucial for it leads, ultimately, to a consolidation of the social order. In 'The Guilty Vicarage' (*Harper's Magazine*, 1948), W.H. Auden highlights the collective dimension of this individual, usually solitary, act: 'Murder is unique in that it abolishes the party it injures, so that society has to take the place of the victim and on his behalf demand restitution or grant forgiveness; it is the one crime in which society has a direct interest.' Despite being furnished with the accoutrements of modernity, the world of the whodunit is tight-knit, hierarchical, and resistant to change. A spot of killing is just the ticket to shake up this cosy conformity and put it to the test. From this perspective, the victim appears as a scapegoat, whose sacrifice is necessary to uphold the community's values, while the murderer – whose capture and punishment mark the restoration of order – is unwittingly in cahoots with the system.

And what of the detective? I hear you ask. One could argue that the detective embodies what Michel Foucault calls the author function ('What is an Author?', 1969). In his famous lecture, the French philosopher contends that the function of the author is to put an end to the dizzying proliferation of textual meaning: this is what the novelist intended and so this is what their book means – end of story. In a similar way, detectives put an end to the proliferation of accusations tearing the community apart by producing a univocal version of the truth. Their task is obviously to outwit culprits and bring them to justice, but in making sense of seemingly baffling clues, they also manage to render the world legible again. A spade is a spade, they explain, even when used as a lethal weapon. In a sense, language is returned to its Adamic condition, as though no gap existed between word and world, signifier and signified – take that Saussure! Significantly, Auden presents the appeal of this genre (its 'phantasy') in Biblical terms. Murder is the original sin, 'the act of disruption by which innocence is lost'. The detective's mission, thereafter, is precisely 'to restore the state of grace': 'The phantasy, then, which the detective story addict indulges is the phantasy of being restored to the Garden of Eden, to a state of innocence, where he may know love as love and not as the law.'

Edgar Allan Poe referred to his crime fiction – in which C. Auguste Dupin deploys preternatural feats of deduction – as 'tales of ratiocination'. In Conan Doyle's *The Sign of the Four* (1890), Sherlock Holmes tells Dr Watson that '[d]etection is, or ought to be, an exact science and should be treated in the same cold and unemotional manner... The only point in the case [*A Study in Scarlet*] which deserved mention was the curious analytical reasoning from effects to causes, by which I succeeded in unravelling it.' W.H. Auden, in the aforementioned essay, describes Holmes as 'a genius in whom scientific curiosity is raised to the status of a heroic passion' and his methods as being akin to 'those of the chemist or physicist'. Such detectives have inherited the cult of science of the naturalist novelists of the late nineteenth century. Their quasi-fanatical faith in reason mirrors their creators' unshakeable belief in narrative and metaphor as modes of epistemological enquiry. In *City of Glass* (1985), the first part of his postmodern noir *New York Trilogy*, Paul Auster riffs on this commonplace parallel between detective and writer: 'The detective is the one who looks, listens, who moves through this morass of objects and events in search of the thought, the idea that will pull all of these things together and make sense of them. In effect, the writer and the detective are interchangeable.' Indeed they are: both are looking for a neat story that will conveniently explain everything. This, however, is not true to life, as the businessman puts it to the private eye in Raymond Chandler's *The Lady in the Lake* (1943): 'Look here, Marlowe, I think I can understand your detective instinct to tie everything that happens into one compact knot, but don't let it run away with you. Life isn't like that at all – not life as I have known it.'

In 'The Simple Act of Murder' (*Atlantic Monthly*, 1944), Chandler famously praised Dashiell Hammett's gritty realism as an antidote to the quaint, antiquated English whodunit. The hardboiled genre occupies a totally different territory – American, urban, modern, sleazy – but it produces its own conventions, which are as far removed from 'reality' as those of, say, Agatha Christie. One could flag up the cult of the individual (the wisecracking sleuth as latter-day knight errant or urban cowboy), the highly stylised epigrammatic dialogue, or the multiplication of murders, which appear even more inconsequential than in the genteel whodunits of yore. For life as we know it (or perhaps rather as we do not know it) I recommend you consult Georges Perec's *Life: A User's Manual* (1978), where Bartlebooth dies clutching the last piece of a jigsaw puzzle –

that turns out to be the wrong shape. If life is a puzzle, it is an unsolvable one.

What we could loosely call postmodern or metafictional detective stories tend to eschew neat conclusions. The prime example is Thomas Pynchon's *The Crying of Lot 49* (1965), which ends, tantalisingly, just as the mystery is about to be revealed. These are the last two sentences: 'The auctioneer cleared his throat. Oedipa settled back, to await the crying of lot 49.' Raymond Roussel (1877–1933) obviously predates the very concept of postmodernism by a long chalk, but his curious work provides an interesting counterexample. Here, as Alain Robbe-Grillet has pointed out, the reader is given such extravagantly elaborate explanations 'that it is as if the mystery remained intact': 'We have the impression of having found a locked drawer, then a key; and this key opens the drawer quite perfectly – but the drawer is empty.' In Franz Kafka's *The Trial* (1925), there is a guilty party (Josef K.) but, ostensibly at least, no crime. In Jorge Luis Borges's short story 'Death and the Compass' (1942), the detective discovers where the last of a series of crimes will take place only to become the victim.

A hallmark of this subgenre is the detective as semiotician or semiologist – as interpreter of signs. Gilbert Adair's *The Death of the Novel* (1992) is a satire of Paul de Man, the controversial Belgian literary theorist, that morphs progressively into a murder mystery. In *The 7th Function of Language* (2015), Laurent Binet imagines that French post-structuralist Roland Barthes did not die following an accident in 1980, but was in fact murdered: a young academic specialising in semiology is recruited to guide the police inspector through the arcane world of Theory. The semiologist-detective is simply an extension of the detective as amateur scientist of the early twentieth century. Both figures read the world like a book, but here it is no longer the Book of Nature: the world is now a construct. The only thing that escapes discourse – the only thing that is not written in advance – is death, understood as the locus of the real, which Lacan defines as 'that which is unassimilable by any system of representation'. This, of course, puts a whole new complexion on murder.

Can murder ever be considered legitimate? Jean-Paul Sartre famously clashed with Albert Camus over the subject, the former supporting revolutionary violence (*Dirty Hands*, 1948) while the latter rejected such barbaric methods (*The Just Assassins*, 1949). Fyodor Dostoevsky takes a more metaphysical approach in *Crime and Punishment* (1866), where he ponders the implications of a godless world. Rodion Raskolnikov is an impoverished ex-law student, who convinces himself that he has the right to kill a pawnbroker. After all, she is old, corrupt, and he will be able to use her money to improve his own life and that of others. By killing her, he also wants to prove that he is a superior being – a kind of *Übermensch* – like his hero Napoleon. Prior to this, he had written an article, entitled 'On Crime', in which he stated that humanity is divided into ordinary and extraordinary people. The latter, he argued, were beyond good and evil; unfettered by laws or morals. The murder he goes on to commit can thus be seen as a transition from theory to practice – a misguided attempt, perhaps, to experience the real.

Lafcadio, in André Gide's *The Vatican Cellars* (1914), has serious delusions of grandeur too. Travelling on board a train, he hatches a plan to commit an *acte gratuit* by suddenly opening the carriage door and pushing a random passenger into the void: 'An unmotivated crime, Lafcadio went on to himself: what a hell of a quandary for the police!' Part of the thrill resides in committing the perfect crime and literally getting away with murder. There is also (as with Raskolnikov) the transgressive *jouissance* of not simply thinking the unthinkable, but acting upon it: 'What a distance there is between imagining something and doing it!' The issue at stake, here, is whether a murder can ever be truly unmotivated. Lafcadio is clearly driven by a desire to express the supremacy of his free will. Besides, his victim is not totally random as he had objected to the way the 'old fart' had flashed him a suggestive smile earlier on. In any case, Lafcadio does not consider himself as a criminal at all: 'Crime! The word seemed bizarre, and the word criminal, applied to him, totally inappropriate. He preferred adventurer, a word as flexible as his beaver hat, whose edges could also be reshaped at will.' Note that last dandyish flourish and then consider the *acte gratuit* as the criminal's take on art for art's sake.

Lafcadio's 'unmotivated crime' is reprised in Patrick Hamilton's 1929 play *Rope*, where two Oxford undergraduates murder a fellow student in order to affirm their Nietzschean superiority. They hide the corpse in a chest on which a buffet is later served during a house party to which, perversely, they have invited the victim's friends and family. In Hitchcock's 1948 film, one of the dandies declares, 'Murder can be an art too. The power to kill can be just as satisfying as the power to create… We've killed for the sake of danger and for the sake of killing. We're alive – truly and wonderfully alive.'

This notion of murder as an art form can be traced at least as far back as Thomas De Quincey's parodic essay 'On Murder Considered as One of the Fine Arts' (1827). However, it is Oscar Wilde's 'Pen, Pencil, and Poison: A Study in Green' (1885) that cemented the connection between writer/artist and criminal. The essay is a paean to the 'young dandy' Thomas Griffiths Wainewright, who justified poisoning his sister-in-law by invoking her 'very thick ankles'. He is believed to have been a serial killer – the author praises 'his achievements in the sphere of poison' – and, according to legend, went about town with strychnine concealed in a ring on his finger. Wilde claims that not only is there 'no essential incongruity between crime and culture' but that the former is actually a great asset to the latter: 'His crimes seem to have had an important effect upon his art,' lending 'a strong personality to his style'.

This portrait of the artist as a criminal (or vice versa) may remind us of the enduring fascination with Lacenaire, the writer, dandy (yet another) and serial killer who ended up on the guillotine in 1836, or of Patricia Cornwell's convincing contention that the painter Walter Sickert was none other than Jack the Ripper. In G.K. Chesterton's 'The Blue Cross' (1910), Aristide Valentin – an 'unfathomably French' policeman – regards the criminal as the true 'creative artist' and the detective as 'only the critic'. The association between art, murder and the *Übermensch* recurs in Francis Iles's crime novel *Malice Aforethought*

(1931), where a nerdy husband suddenly feels that he has metamorphosed into a 'fine artist' and a 'superman' after bumping off his wife. As for the criminal dandy, there is a clear lineage linking Wilde's Dorian Gray to Bret Easton Ellis's Patrick Bateman (*American Psycho*, 1991) and Patricia Highsmith's Tom Ripley, whose talents certainly include the art of murder (*The Talented Mr Ripley*, 1955).

It is difficult to overstate the thematic importance of murder for any writer, let alone a crime writer – it is bound up with the mysteries of being and not being, inscription and erasure. Jasper Johns famously described Robert Rauschenberg's *Erased de Kooning Drawing* (1953) as an 'additive subtraction', but could not this be said of all works of art and literature? A painting, according to Picasso, is 'a sum of destructions'. All books are the result of elimination and omission, revision and redaction – killing your darlings (the original phrase, coined by Sir Arthur Quiller-Couch in 1914, was actually '[m]urder your darlings'). Lavinia Greenlaw recounts how her writing is 'shaped by the stories [she] will not tell' (*Some Answers Without Questions*, 2021). 'Destruction was my Beatrice,' declared the poet Stéphane Mallarmé apropos of his writing method.

W.H. Auden's astute definition of murder as 'negative creation' – from which he infers that 'every murderer is therefore the rebel who claims the right to be omnipotent' – could be used to describe the wave of nihilism that spread through European literary and artistic circles at the end of the nineteenth century and the beginning of the twentieth. Len Gutkin views it as a product of 'aestheticism's desire to correct an ugly world': '[i]f the world cannot be made beautiful, it can at least be destroyed,' he explains. It was probably also due to the exaggerated claims made for artists and writers, who were called upon to fill the spiritual vacuum left by the growing secularisation of society. Forced to recognise that *creatio ex nihilo* was beyond their grasp, writers like the Symbolist Marcel Schwob drew the conclusion that the urge to destroy is also 'a creative passion' (Mikhail Bakunin) — and perhaps the only truly human one. As Tom Ripley puts it in Anthony Minghella's 1999 film adaptation, 'If I could take a giant eraser and rub out everything, starting with myself.'

Novelist Deborah Levy has spoken of the 'sheriff's notebook' in which she used to gather 'evidence for something [she] could not fathom' at the time. A crime that was yet to be committed, perhaps, as in Alain Robbe-Grillet's *The Erasers* (1953) — an inversion of the tale of Oedipus — where the detective investigates a murder that is yet to take place and that he will himself come to commit. Unless the evidence gathering itself constituted the crime. After all, the detective is the writer, and like Josef K., the writer is always guilty. Their dirty little secret is the destructive power at the heart of the words they use to create. '[L]anguage is murder,' argues philosopher Simon Critchley, 'that is, the act of naming things, of substituting a name for a sensation, gives things to us, but in a form that deprives those things of their being.'

I accuse Mrs Levy, with the *OED*, in the Library. You can always count on a murderer for a fancy prose style.

Spotlight on...
Patricia Highsmith

No Compromises: The Crime Fiction of Patricia Highsmith

Barry Forshaw

My encounter with one of crime fiction's truly legendary names, Patricia Highsmith, was memorable – to say the least. What's more, it conformed to the image that is most commonly associated with her: that she was a difficult woman, impatient with social niceties, who took no prisoners.

I was in my twenties, and it was at an author's publishing launch in London – though not a launch for one of her own books (she, like me, was a guest). When I spotted an intense-looking woman with sloping shoulders, standing alone in the corner of the room and smoking furiously (as was permissible indoors then), I said to my host, a celebrated editor of crime fiction, 'Surely that's Patricia Highsmith?' When he confirmed with a wry smile that indeed it was, I asked why nobody was talking to her. 'Go and speak to her, Barry,' he replied, 'and you'll see why!'

I gritted my teeth and walked over – I knew her reputation. While remaining resolutely unsmiling for our encounter, she was not unwelcoming after some initial small talk. But then I unwittingly took my life in my hands when I made a reference to the film of her novel *Strangers on a Train*. 'It must have been a hell of an experience,' I said, 'having your first novel filmed by Alfred Hitchcock – from a screenplay part-written by Raymond Chandler!' She glared at me and snapped out her reply: 'They fucked my book!' Finding myself in the position of having to defend the film – one of the director's key American movies – she cut across what I was saying. 'The murder swap of the novel is crucial – take it away, and what have you got? Hitchcock removed it!' I pointed out that the censorship of the day (the early 1950s) would not have had the law-abiding protagonist – the Farley Granger character – committing a murder. But the unforgiving Highsmith was having none of that. What followed in our conversation was a series of polite disagreements over a variety of other topics, including her writing a series of books about a murderer, Tom Ripley, and her attitude to the women killed in her novels (some, she said, deserving it). While it seemed I could say nothing she would agree with, I was keenly aware that I would remember this encounter for the rest of my life.

Patricia Highsmith (whose real name was the less euphonious Mary Patricia Plangman) was born in Fort Worth, Texas, in January 1921 (she died in February 1995). Her writing surname was taken from her adoptive stepfather, whom her mother married after her divorce. Highsmith's creative streak perhaps originated with her biological parents, both artists, Mary and Jay Bernard Plangman, although another less welcome influence on her worldview might have been the fact that her parents divorced only a week or so before Highsmith was born.

Another rather bleak aspect of her biography is the fact that – as Highsmith related – her mother told her she had tried to abort her daughter by swallowing turpentine. Such traumas may have dictated some of Highsmith's early reading choices, including books on Freudian analysis such as *The Human Mind* by Karl Menninger. Graduating from Barnard College (where her chosen subjects included English composition, short story writing and drama), Highsmith was attracted to rebellious, bohemian milieux – and it is perhaps no surprise that over twenty of her novels were set in the geographical centre of such movements, New York's Greenwich Village.

In her early attempts to become a writer, she made applications to such prestigious publications as *Harper's Bazaar*, *Vogue* and *Good Housekeeping*. All of them summarily turned her down, but she was successful in one particular area, a less-than-respectable market she worked in along with fellow crime writer Mickey Spillane: Highsmith wrote American comic books. In later life, she kept relatively quiet about this aspect of her career, perhaps because she was writing in a time when comics were the target of self-appointed censors who regarded them as horrendous attacks on American decency and Christian life. One might have thought that such a vaguely anti-establishment field as comics would appeal to the taboo-busting writer, but that does not take into account the literary respectability she was to acquire later and the fact that comics had yet to be taken seriously as cultural artefacts. It is perhaps significant that her creation of adventures for superheroes – with their concealed double lives – can be seen as a kind of rough-hued training for her later endeavours, in which hidden identities are par for the course.

In terms of her personal life, Highsmith acknowledged a drinking problem, and she had difficulty sustaining long-term relationships, possibly because, on occasion, she pursued straight women – and even sometimes had short-term affairs with them. As a gay woman who occasionally had sexual encounters with men, she often remarked about preferring the company of men to her own sex (something else she and I discussed). However, she claimed to prefer animals over human beings – a predilection she shared with the actress Brigitte Bardot. The US editor Otto Penzler (one of her publishers) told me he was amazed that someone with such a negative view of the human race could still write so perceptively about characters often quite unlike herself – although there is customarily a misanthropic character in most of her books. As for her work ethic, it was undeniably impressive – and not just in terms of the finished, published novels; she also toiled at ideas for unwritten books, articles, short story ideas and even thirty-eight writer's notebooks and diaries. She also sketched, painted and made sculptures, activities that she continued during her English sojourn when living in Suffolk; it was there that she wrote a key novel, *A Suspension of Mercy*, discussed below.

Patricia Highsmith is now perceived as the darkest and most misanthropic of crime writers, with a notably jaundiced view of the human race – including of her own sex. (While a feminist of sorts, Highsmith would have had no truck with the notion of women being the superior sex.) But of all crime writers, male and female, her cool, existential view of the cruel way in which human beings behave to one another seems most in tune with the more psychologically astute practitioners of the crime writer's art. Certainly, she would not belong to such trends as the kind of fiction offering a comforting view of humanity, but her recurrent suggestion that all of us have the capacity for violence and malfeasance with the right provocation or temptation seems aligned with a similar view of human nature to be found in the work of such literary writers as Albert Camus and Joseph Conrad.

Another literary writer who prefigured her work was Henry James (1843–1916). Like James, Highsmith was an American with a notably unromantic view of her own country – and, again like James, she chose to live in Europe while fashioning a series of characters who were regarded by their creator with an Olympian detachment, whatever their behaviour. Highsmith allowed readers to make up their own mind about the morality or otherwise of her protagonists.

She inaugurated her career with the remarkable *Strangers on a Train* in 1950 and almost immediately gained the respect and admiration of her peers. This is still one of the great debut novels in crime fiction, as disturbing and off-kilter as anything in the genre. What makes the book's achievement particularly noteworthy is the fact that her talent seemed to arrive in a polished and finished state; unlike, say, Graham Greene (a great admirer of her work – notably of her diamond-hard short stories), there was no sense of her having to grow into the genre. All of the uncompromising elements that distinguished Highsmith's later work are to be found in this first book. Two men have a chance encounter on a train. Architect Guy Haines is a stand-in for the reader. He appears to have a normal if unhappy life, trapped in a dead marriage with the less-than-likeable Miriam. But the other stranger on the train happens to be a psychopath: Charles Anthony Bruno, coded by Highsmith as homosexual (with a possible unacknowledged attraction between the two men). Bruno reflects certain aspects of Guy Haines's personality but is otherwise his polar opposite. In an exchange that Guy initially assumes isn't serious, Bruno suggests a swapping of murders: he will kill Miriam if Guy will perform a similar termination of Bruno's hated father. But Guy subsequently realises that the proposal was no joke, and that Bruno has in fact murdered Miriam. Then begins the real business of the novel: the psychological battle in which Bruno insists that Guy completes his part of the bargain – and commit murder. As noted above, the censorship of the day meant that Alfred Hitchcock's film had to diverge sharply from the novel, and Guy manages to escape the consequences of the deal he made in jest. But in Highsmith's novel, Guy is obliged by the non-stop assaults and threats of the deranged Bruno to actually commit the murder. The novel is the first example in the writer's work of the queasy moral equivocation that she became famous for – and the way in which the reader changes their mind about the seemingly conventional Guy is a test of the reader's own moral position.

There are those, however, who regard her signature books as those featuring the amoral confidence trickster and murderer Tom Ripley; the first, *The Talented Mr Ripley* (1955), and the subsequent *Ripley Under Ground* (1970) are reader favourites. In the conversation I had with Highsmith, I asked her how she maintained her level of inspiration when writing a series of books about a psychopath. 'Who are you talking about?' she replied, her expression unchanged. 'If you mean Tom Ripley, he is *not* a psychopath – he simply kills people who get in his way.' The views (possibly tongue-in-cheek) of Ripley's creator notwithstanding, there is no arguing with the fact that Ripley is a serial killer – as may be ascertained by the body count that can be ascribed to him over the course of five books.

In *The Talented Mr Ripley*, readers are introduced to Tom Ripley, who initially appears as an ineffectual young man leading the life of a con man. He is hired by the moneyed Herbert Greenleaf to track down his son, the high-living Dickie. Ripley finds Dickie in Italy, all the while corresponding with Greenleaf Senior. But the attraction of Dickie's sybaritic lifestyle is too great for him, and a violent act follows. Ripley assumes Dickie Greenleaf's identity himself, and maintains the fiction by writing to the latter's friends and associates, but avoiding their company. More criminal acts follow, and the book has a strange dual effect on the receptive reader: we may be repelled by the amoral Ripley, but we find ourselves (against our better judgement) wanting him to succeed in his criminal enterprises.

Those familiar with the writing of Henry James (as namechecked above) will recognise the inspiration for the narrative here: James's *The Ambassadors* (1903) also focuses on a protagonist who is sent to rescue an American who has gone astray abroad. However, there are signal differences between the two writers: James's Lambert Strether is not a murderer, and while James and Highsmith – both Europe-based Americans – similarly use American expats as protagonists, Highsmith seems to relish the destruction of her innocents abroad. In subsequent books, Ripley is enjoying the high life in France with a seductive partner, following his principal hobby: the acquisition of fine art. The latter, of course, requires the acquisition of funds, and we watch with grim fascination as Ripley employs a variety of ruthless means to obtain them. One heartless tactic, for instance, can be found in *Ripley's Game* (1974), in which he persuades a vulnerable man that he does not have long to live with a view to getting him to commit a crime. Similarly, in *The Boy Who Followed Ripley* (1980), Ripley draws a young man into a world of criminality.

Throughout the series, it becomes clear to Highsmith's fascinated readers (including, as mentioned above, Graham Greene, who was an admirer of the Ripley sequence) that Highsmith is not in the business of critiquing her murderous antihero. The fact that Ripley became a signature character for her was partly due to the number of films made of the books; taken together, they present a fascinatingly varied series of portrayals of Tom Ripley – from Alain Delon in *Plein Soleil* (the 1960 film version of *The Talented Mr Ripley*, directed by René Clément) and Dennis Hopper in *Der Amerikanische Freund*, director Wim Wenders' 1977 version of *Ripley's Game*, to, perhaps most significantly, Matt Damon in Anthony Minghella's handsome and persuasive remake of *The Talented Mr Ripley* (1999). Damon conveyed perfectly the novel's transformation of Ripley from an unpractised chancer into a ruthless killer. (At the time of writing, filming is finished on a new Netflix series with Andrew Scott as Ripley.)

Highsmith also forged a model of the standalone novel that was very much her own. Such non-series novels as *A Suspension of Mercy* (1965) and *This Sweet Sickness* (1960) avoided the notion of detectives as protagonists – a device that clearly had no appeal for her – and usher us into a world in which the psyches of her characters are preserved in a carefully maintained balance that is steadily disrupted, usually by their own ill-considered actions.

But perhaps the most significant contribution that Highsmith made to the crime genre is her modern inauguration of the 'domestic noir' idiom, with its issues of betrayal in heterosexual relationships, although she avoids the standard tropes of the genre (the male sex being the repository of all violence, and females as vulnerable, deluded victims) –

Highsmith, in contrast, casts a cold eye over the whole human race, disregarding gender. The line of succession in the psychological suspense novel is a lengthy and tortuous one, but such talents in the field as Ruth Rendell would happily admit to the minatory influence of Highsmith (in fact, Rendell was often described as a British heir apparent of her American predecessor, not least for her singularly unsparing view of the human condition). The level of psychological acuity and dark menace in Highsmith's work was invariably set in prose that had the air of being refined to within an inch of its life; the crime genre – reservoir of so much dull and by-the-numbers writing – was enriched by Highsmith's contribution.

A Suspension of Mercy (1965), written in Britain, is a typical example of Highsmith's work in this field. The central premise is of a man who is considering the murder of his wife. Sydney Bartleby (his surname borrowed from another American writer of distinction, Herman Melville) is obsessed with assembling a variety of ways in which he might kill his spouse and supply a perfect alibi. As a writer of thrillers, he is well disposed to formulate such morbid notions, but when his wife goes missing, he finds that he cannot persuade anyone that he is not behind her disappearance. Few modern writers describing a poisonous male–female relationship would be prepared to move into such dark areas of the psyche as Highsmith does here, but she is completely at home in this territory, as much as she is in the levels of misdirection she throws at the reader.

Another novel of psychological suspense that Highsmith wrote in Suffolk was *Those Who Walk Away* (1967), and the narrative roller coaster that the novel takes the reader on is one of her most unsettling. When Peggy Garrett commits suicide, her death ruptures the lives of two men, her husband and her father, both of whom lay the blame for her death at the feet of the other. The dead woman's husband, Ray Garrett, finds himself pursued by Ed Coleman, her father, who is a painter. A grim – and decidedly peripatetic – game of cat and mouse ensues: violence and pursuit take place in Venice and Rome. Like many of Highsmith's narratives, there is never a sense of the clichéd here, and even readers familiar with the author's work will find themselves defeated when trying to predict plot developments.

The Glass Cell (1964) was another novel that Highsmith completed during her Suffolk sojourn. It came about when Highsmith corresponded with a convict in America who had contacted her to tell her how taken he had been with her novel *Deep Water* (1957). The central figure here is another criminal antihero, Philip Carter, who, like Tom Ripley, has an appreciation of high culture while being prepared to get his hands dirty in acts of criminality. Like several other Highsmith heroes, he has a low sex drive – perhaps diverting the erotic into other more challenging activities. At the start of the novel, Carter has been accused of a crime he hasn't committed and has been wrongfully imprisoned. When he is released, he kills his wife's lover, finally adapting readily to the new life that murder has presented him with. The 'glass cell' of the title is the prison that Carter himself will carry around for the rest of his life – even though, as usual, Highsmith is not in a hurry to judge him.

After her time in Suffolk and the breakup of a love affair (during which she compiled, among other things, a notebook that was a gallery of bad art), Highsmith fled across France and Switzerland, her problems with alcoholism deepening and a series of doomed love affairs invariably self-destructing. Despite these distractions, her work productivity remained as prodigious as ever, and she continued to write in the impressive modernist house in the Ticino that was to be her final domicile. Her death came about in a bizarre and piquant way – one that the author herself found grimly fascinating even as it wrecked her body. She died of two diseases that were competing in her body – and doctors told her that neither one could be treated without making the other worse. However, unlike other self-loathing American masters of the crime novel, such as Cornell Woolrich, Highsmith lived to see her work become greatly admired, and she was particularly proud of the esteem in which she was held by writers who moved in more literary territories.

Even admirers of Patricia Highsmith will readily admit that she was a caustic and often unpleasant character (including being relatively virulently antisemitic); however, it is probably impossible to separate the writer's remarkably jaundiced vision from the compelling narratives in which she placed her characters. In the third decade of the twenty-first century, there has been a considerable revival in what is called on both sides of the Atlantic 'cosy crime' ('cosy mysteries' in the US), in which murder is committed simply to provide a plot hook – the very notion that Raymond Chandler loathed in the novels of the British Golden Age of crime fiction. Such writing – despite its massive appeal – would have been anathema to Highsmith, who essentially presented her own dystopian perception of the way in which human beings behave. Perhaps in her refusal to condemn, she was closer to such non-genre writers as Albert Camus, whose *L'Étranger/The Outsider* (1942) similarly allows us to examine the crimes committed by its central character without any overt authorial commentary. And, in many ways, this aspect of Highsmith's writing – as much as the finely honed elegance of her prose – made her a writer for the ages. There is no question that her legacy and influence will continue unabated.

The Motive

Authors write for a variety of reasons. For some, it is the simple pleasure in chiselling a story from the raw materials, pulling a living story into being by sheer imagination. For others, it is the drive to dramatise social issues, to use plot, characters and narrative to present readers with an authentic picture of the world, one that may contribute to effecting real social change. Indeed, many writers write without having a clear sense of their motivation, a compulsion which, like a great many murderers, they simply cannot name.

The following essays present a range of responses to the questions 'why write?' and 'why crime?', but the interrogation needn't end there. There are as many motives for writing as there are writers, and there's no guarantee you'll end up where you expected. Sometimes there's a twist in the ending.

There's Been a Murder: Miscarriages of Justice, Respectability and the Fatal Flaw

Louise Welsh

I live in the Square Mile of Murder, something late-night taxi drivers often tell me, just before I step from their cab into the dimly lit street. The phrase was coined in the 1960s by Jack House, aka Mr Glasgow, a popular journalist and chronicler of the city, who used it as the title for his best-known book.[1] The Square Mile begins with a passage that may owe something to George Orwell's 'Decline of the English Murder':

> All the best Glasgow murders have taken place in the West End in the spring or summer. Not only that, but Glasgow can boast (if that is the right word) that four of

---
1 Jack House, *Square Mile of Murder, Horrific Glasgow Killings* (Black & White Publishing, 1961).

the world's greatest murder cases took part within one square mile of the city.[2]

House goes on to speculate that other places such as 'the Notting Hill[3] district of London might well have a square mile that could beat Glasgow's in quantity. But when it comes to quality' he is adamant that our city is world beating in the murder department.

Out of the four murders House examines, it is the Oscar Slater case that interests me most. On 21 December 1908, sometime after 6 p.m., Helen Lambie, a young maidservant, slipped out of the first-floor flat at 15 Queens Terrace, as she did most evenings, to fetch a newspaper for her employer, eighty-two-year-old Miss Marion Gilchrist. She returned at around 7 p.m. to find the downstairs neighbour, Mr Adams, at the door to Miss Gilchrist's flat. He had been worried by

---

2   The cases referred to are Madeleine Smith (tried in 1857), Jessie McLachlan (1862), Dr Pritchard aka The Human Crocodile (1865) & Oscar Slater (1909).

3   Jack House makes this comparison glibly. The Notting Hill riots took place in 1958, three years before the publication of *Square Mile of Murder*. At that time Notting Hill was a poor area of London. The riots were a response to racism and police targeting of people of colour and their businesses. A leaflet issued by the Afro-Asian West Indian Union in the same year states, 'A young man from the West Indies, Kelso Cochrane, has been murdered. He was not a criminal. He harmed nobody. But he was black. It seems he had to pay for that.' The leaflet goes on to recount other outrages and issues an instruction to 'ORGANISE, ORGANISE, ORGANISE!... evil has to be fought but it must be fought in an *organised* way.' The question of what makes 'a good murder', a crime worthy of investigation, is one we will return to. Warwick Digital Collections, To the coloured citizens of West London, cdm21047.contentdm.oclc.org/digital/collection/tav/id/4919.

the sound of a disturbance. Mr Adams had rung the bell several times but although the gas lamps were lit inside the flat, there was no other sign of life. Helen unlocked[4] and opened the door and a smartly dressed man walked from the spare bedroom, past Mr Adams, down the stairs and out of the building.[5] Mr Adams got the impression that Helen knew the man and was about to speak to him, but he escaped 'like greased lightening'. The pair went inside and found Miss Gilchrist bloody and battered on the floor of the drawing

---

[4] The locked doors add to the mystery. There were three locks on the door. Two of them were turned. The third was only used when the occupants retired for the night.

[5] This detail reminds me of a poem by William Ernest Henley, 'Madam Life's a Piece in Bloom' (1920):

Madam Life's a piece in bloom
Death goes dogging everywhere:
She's the tenant of the room,
He's the ruffian on the stair.

You shall see her as a friend,
You shall bilk him once or twice;
But he'll trap you in the end,
And he'll stick you for her price.

With his kneebones at your chest,
And his knuckles in your throat,
You would reason – plead – protest!
Clutching at her petticoat;

But she's heard it all before,
Well she knows you've had your fun,
Gingerly she gains the door,
And your little job is done.

room. She died moments later without being able to tell them what had happened. Mr Adams ran after the intruder, but he had disappeared.

The crime is not remembered by the name of its victim, Miss Marion Gilchrist, but by that of Oscar Slater, the man who was wrongly convicted of the murder and served eighteen and a half years in Peterhead Prison. I live on the street where Miss Gilchrist used to live. I walk by her tenement most days and the crime flits through my mind every time I pass it.

This one of the ways in which the criminal ley lines of cities work. Here is the building where the old lady was battered to death, this is the stretch of canal where the jogger was fatally stabbed, there is the nightclub where the girl was last seen, down there the stretch of park where the woman's body was found, this is the alleyway where he stuffed her into a dustbin...[6]

In the early sixties, when House wrote *Square Mile of Murder*, Glasgow was popularly viewed as a dark industrial

---

[6] Writing this reminded me of Kei Miller's poetry collection *in nearby bushes* (Carcanet, 2019) which takes its title from the place perpetrators are repeatedly described as escaping into in Jamaica, the bush or hills. The collection employs accounts of murders from actual news and court reports. Bodies are also found 'in nearby bushes' an unnamed place marked by death. Miller writes:

> To consider the nearby bushes – a stretch of cornfield perhaps, or the crotons behind the house – is to consider the nameless places, or perhaps the placeless places. It is to consider the nonspecific 'here' – a here that could be everywhere, or maybe nowhere.

city, home to hardmen and razor gangs. House blames its violent reputation on journalists' enthusiasm for reporting crime[7] and quotes an anonymous 'authority' as stating, 'you've only got to flash a razor in Glasgow to get onto the front page'. House suggests that, on the contrary, as in Robert Louis Stevenson's *The Strange Case of Dr Jekyll and Mr Hyde*, an intense regard for respectability underpinned the world in which the murders were carried out. Except for Dr Pritchard, the Human Crocodile,[8] the Square Mile cases are also linked by uncertainties about their verdicts.[9] An uncertainty which

---

7   House may be thinking of the novel *No Mean City* by Alexander McArthur and Kingsley Long (1935), starring Johnnie Stark the 'Razor King' of the Gorbals. The Mitchell Library's website describes it as a 'grim tale of violence, gang fights, drunkenness' which 'gave Glasgow, and Gorbals in particular, an image which it has struggled to live down ever since'. It is worth noting that Glasgow libraries refused to stock the novel when it first came out. Professor Willy Maley of Glasgow University describes *No Mean City* as a 'cutting edge portrait of working-class life in the worst laid scheme in Scotland' (*100 Best Scottish Books*, 2005). The book gave its title to the theme tune of STV's Glasgow cop drama *Taggart* written by Mike Moran and sung by Maggie Bell (1992). Mark McManus starred as Jim Taggart from 1983 until his death in 1994. The series coined the catchphrase, 'There's been a murder.'

8   Edward William Pritchard was the last person to be hanged in public in Scotland. Reportedly around one 100,000 people turned out on Glasgow Green on 18 July 1865 to witness his execution. It was a Friday and Glasgow loves a party. Pritchard was a strange case who murdered his wife, mother-in-law and probably a young, female servant. Before suspicion fell on him, he appeared devastated by his wife's death, insisting the lid of her coffin be unscrewed so that he could kiss her lips one last time. His crocodile tears earned him the nickname of the Human Crocodile.

9   In the case of Madeleine Smith, who was accused of killing her lover, the jury decided on a 'not proven' verdict. The popular jury is still out on Madeleine Smith, and you can read many articles stating or disputing her innocence. Jessie McLachlan insisted she was innocent of the murder of Jessie McPherson in the Sandyford Murder Case. She was found guilty and

in Oscar Slater's case was corrected when he was declared innocent.[10]

Oscar Slater was German and Jewish, a dapper man in a city where men who were interested in their appearance were considered suspect.[11] His real name, Oscar Leschziner, was difficult for English speakers to get their teeth around, and for that, and possibly other reasons, he used multiple names – Sando, George, Anderson, Schmidt and Slater, the name he was best known by in Glasgow. Slater made his living as a bookie, a dealer in jewellery, a gymnastics instructor, and a dentist (!). It was also rumoured that he may have been a pimp. So far, so very foreign to the air of respectability allegedly coveted by the citizens of Glasgow's West End.[12]

---

sentenced to death by hanging. After a public outcry, McLachlan's sentence was commuted to life imprisonment. She served fifteen years in Perth Prison before being released and emigrating to the United States.

10   As Jack House notes, the best source is William Roughead's *The Trial of Oscar Slater*, part of the Notable British Trials series. The first edition, published in 1910, only two years after the murder of Miss Gilchrist, explored worrying aspects of Slater's conviction.

11   Graham Hoey of Hoey's Department store recalls that working men delegated the buying of their clothes, except for their caps (bunnets), to their wives. It was considered unmanly to show any preference of taste. If a man needed a new cap, he 'opened the door and still keeping your hand on the handle of the door, you said, "A bunnet", and somebody gave you one and you put it on your head and said, "Aye that's fine" and gave your 1/11*d* or whatever it was and got out the door as quickly as possible!' *Up Oor Close. Memories of Domestic Life in Glasgow Tenements 1910–1945*, Jean Faley (White Cockade, 1990).

12   At the beginning of the nineteenth century Glasgow's city centre was becoming overcrowded and unsanitary. People who could afford to began to move west. Miss Gilchrist's property at Queen's Terrace, now West Princes Street, was a desirable address. The area around West Princes Street declined in

Slater lodged in St George's Road, round the corner from Miss Gilchrist's flat. The old lady was reputed to have a collection of valuable jewellery. Five days after the murder, Slater sailed for New York. Witnesses said that before he left, he attempted to sell a pawn ticket for a diamond brooch. So far, so circumstantial…

Miscarriages of justice have been part of crime fiction from the start. William Godwin's *Caleb Williams* or *Things as They Are* (1794)[13] opens with a cry to the heavens that Oscar Slater, and other unjustly convicted prisoners from Robben Island to Guantanamo Bay and beyond would recognise:

> My life has for several years been a theatre of calamity. I have been a mark for the vigilance of tyranny, and I could not escape. My fairest prospects have been blasted. My enemy has shown himself inaccessible to entreaties, and untired in persecution. My fame, as well as my happiness, has become his victim. Every one, as far as my story has been known, has refused to assist me in my

---

the 1970s and '80s. The mines and quarries of the old Blythswood estates on which it was built began to let themselves be known, and banks and building societies considered the buildings a poor risk. This made it difficult to buy or sell property. Prices slumped, rogue landlords moved in and the area fell into decline. A series of improvements combined with community activism have helped to restore the area, but West Princes Street and adjacent streets continue to suffer from slum landlords and HMOs. The bricks and mortar are the same, but Miss Gilchrist might be unpleasantly surprised at the state of her old building were she to return.

13   The novel is a fictional companion to Godwin's 1793 political treatise *Enquiry Concerning Political Justice and its Influence on Morals and Happiness.*

distress, and has execrated my name. I have not deserved this treatment.

The novel starts as a kind of detective story. Eighteen-year-old Caleb is from humble beginnings. His mother and father are both dead and he is all alone in the world. Nevertheless, he is a bright boy and secures a good position as secretary to Ferdinando Falkland, the local squire, a man of 'considerable opulence'. Remember this setup. We will meet it again. Caleb has a flaw common to a lot of crime fiction heroes. His nose bothers him, and he does not know when to leave well alone.

Caleb Williams suspects his master murdered his rival, Tyrell. He roots around in Falkland's library and discovers incriminating documents. Eventually, Falkland confesses his guilt. He murdered Tyrell and stood by while two innocent men hung for the crime that he himself had committed.

If *Caleb Williams* were a straightforward detective novel, this might be the final chapter – the culprit identified, punishment to be decided, the structure of the social environment restored. Instead, Squire Falkland's confession is the prelude for a new stage in the novel, his relentless persecution of Caleb. What follows is a series of imprisonments, escapes, adventures and misadventures in which Caleb is ruthlessly stalked and in fear of his life.

Falkland's respectability – his reputation for decency – is the shield that allows him to behave despicably without suffering any consequences. The poor person may be clever, they may be an upstanding citizen, but that is not enough to protect them from the forces of wealth and state, should they combine against them. Caleb Williams is a man, but he might as well be a woman like Emily, for all the protection the law gives him against Falkland's tyranny. This is, as Godwin's alternative title tells us, *Things as They Are*.[14]

Caleb Williams's unfortunate circumstances are echoed in John Grisham's bestselling legal thriller *The Firm* (1991).[15] Mitch McDeere is also from humble beginnings. His mother suffers from poor mental health and he was brought up by his brother Ray, who is now in jail for manslaughter. With the help of his wife Abby, Mitch has managed to beat the odds and put himself through Harvard Law School, where he graduated third in his class. His ambition is to make a lot of money. Mitch's hard work seems about to be rewarded when he is approached by a small Memphis firm, Bendini, Lambert and Locke. They make him an offer he cannot refuse – a fabulous salary, fast track to promotion, and Mitch's choice of car. Mitch does not seem to be aware of the phrase, 'if it looks too good to be true it probably is'. *The Firm* is not a supernatural novel, but it is a deal-with-the-devil story, even though Mitch is unaware of the devil's involvement when he signs the pact.

---

14   Godwin was well versed on the inequalities facing women. His wife, Mary Wollstonecraft, is the author of *A Vindication of the Rights of Woman* (1792). A cornerstone of feminism, the book argues, among other things, for equality of educational opportunities for women and men. Mary Wollstonecraft was in the process of writing a fictional companion to *Vindication of the Rights of Woman*, a novel entitled *Maria* or *The Wrongs of Woman*, when she died in 1797 of puerperal fever following the birth of their daughter, Mary Wollstonecraft Shelley.

15   *The Firm* was adapted into an equally successful movie of the same name, starring Tom Cruise and Gene Hackman (1993).

Mitch has barely arrived in Memphis when two colleagues die in an accident. He notices memorial plaques to three other lawyers who also died in sudden accidents. The title of the book, *The Firm*,[16] gains extra resonance when Mitch is approached by the FBI, who reveal that Bendini, Lambert and Locke are a branch of the Morolto Mafia family. Seventy-five per cent of their business involves tax evasion and money laundering. The dead lawyers were each trying to extricate themselves when the accidents that killed them occurred.

A façade of respectability enables Bendini, Lambert and Locke to conceal their crimes, in the same way that Falkland's wealth and respectability shields him. But Mitch differs from Caleb in several ways. Mitch is not alone. He has a wife he loves (despite casually betraying her on a beach in the Caymans) and a brother who supports him. His misadventures take place not in muddy, rural England but against the chrome and steel of Memphis's business district and the bright waters of the Cayman Islands.[17] The world of Caleb Williams is monocultural. There are peasants and aristocrats, no hint of cultural or racial diversity. Mitch's world is also predominately white and male. But in this case that is a fact that might help alert the reader that all is not well.

John Grisham was born in Jonesboro, Arkansas. He studied and practised law in Mississippi. In the spirit of 'write about

---

16 'The Firm' is also the unofficial nickname for the British Royal Family and its mechanisms. The phrase was coined by King George VI and is affectionately used by the royal family.

17 At one particularly desperate point, poor Caleb, who is starving, is forced to dig a turnip from the mud with his bare hands and gnaw on it raw.

what you know', it makes sense that he sends Mitch McDeere to a Southern law firm. The action of *The Firm* is mainly divided between Memphis and the Cayman Islands. The history of both places offers an extra dimension to *The Firm* should we care to look for it.

The economy of the antebellum South relied on the forced labour of hundreds of thousands of enslaved people, who were originally transported against their will from Africa. Memphis was home to the South's largest slave market, situated in the centre of town on Adams Street, where thousands were bought and sold into misery for the sake of financial profit. The market was operated by Nathan Bedford Forrest (1821–1877), Confederate General and the first Grand Wizard of the Ku Klux Klan.[18] The Cayman Islands are a tax haven in the Caribbean.[19] They too have a history of slavery and are home to many direct descendants of enslaved African people.[20]

The firm of Bendini, Lambert and Locke is exclusively white, heterosexual and male. Mitch is told that they tried hiring a woman once, but it did not work out – she is featured

---

18   The Ku Klux Klan, a notorious white supremacist terror hate group, was first established in 1865. Nathan Bedford Forrest joined in 1867. In 1871 he denied that he had been a member to a congressional hearing.

19   The Cayman Islands is a British Overseas Territory. It was a Jamaican dependency until Jamaican independence in 1962.

20   My own city, Glasgow, has concrete connections with the North Atlantic slave trade. I do not know where Miss Gilchrist's money came from, but much of the wealth that enabled fine houses to be built in the west of the city in the eighteenth century originated from cotton, tobacco and sugar plantations worked by enslaved Africans. Glasgow's involvement with the trade is in the mortar of buildings and institutions across the city.

on one of the plaques commemorating the dead lawyers. It is never stated, but the focused self-interest of the firm means it is dedicated not only to making money for the mob, but to perpetuating male and white supremacy. Poverty features here as a lever.[21] The door to power and riches is open should Mitch wish to walk through (though it is true that the FBI are leaning against it, upping the stakes). By rejecting the offer to join the big boys, Mitch turns himself into a moving target.

Conspiracies to maintain white, male power elites that were themselves forged through slavery, landgrabs, empire and other crimes[22] is a repeated theme in crime fiction. Hard work and ability are not enough. *The Brotherhood of the Bell* suggests that alliances are essential if one wishes to be successful.

Glenn Ford plays Professor Andrew Patterson, a bigshot professor of socioeconomics at the Institute for the Study of Human Civilisation (as unlikely a profession for a high-octane movie hero as tax lawyer). We meet Patterson at dawn as he revisits his Fraternity House to stand as mentor for a new initiate into the Brotherhood of the Bell, a secret society he has been a member of for over twenty years. The ceremony involves three participants – the initiate, his mentor and the mentor's mentor – swearing an oath on their 'fortune, honour and life' before taking turns to ring the ceremonial bell. The

---

21 This is an uncomfortable sex scene involving a mixed-race prostitute who Mitch thinks is attracted to him. Photos of the encounter are used in an attempt to blackmail Mitch into staying loyal to the firm.

22 I use the word 'crimes' in the knowledge that North Atlantic slavery, many landgrabs and empire were within the law at the time they took place.

bell hangs, like a massive Japanese hand grenade,[23] above a brilliant oriental carpet. It is tolled with the aid of a beam of wood which the brothers dunt against its side. After the ceremony, the initiate tells Patterson, 'It's just occurred to me, we're part of the establishment now.' The professor replies, 'Not part. We *are* the establishment.'

The world of *The Brotherhood of the Bell* resembles an American real estate advert from the period. Lawns are mowed, elegant rooms boast sprays of flowers, men are suited, women tasteful. Bookcases are lined with matching bindings which suggest sets of encyclopaedias or Reader's Digest condensed books. Nothing is fun. The trappings of success seem dull, cocktails and good cuisine, rounds of golf with golfish men. Once again there is no LGBTQ+ element or people of colour. It would be reductive to conclude that this is why the brotherhood's world is lacking in style. Queers and PoC do not work exclusively in fashion or interior design, but there is a correlation. Despite its apparent solidity, the dark wood furniture, Silvikrin-set hairdos, and black limousines, this is a fragile environment founded on lies and coercion. There is no room for deviation from a WASPish[24] norm.

As they leave, Professor Patterson's mentor passes him a card and instructs him to visit the address written on it before he flies home. The address turns out to be an empty suburban house which is up for sale. There an anonymous man gives Patterson a sealed envelope. His mission is to prevent his

---

23   I have no real idea what one of these would look like.

24   WASP = White Anglo Saxon Protestants.

close friend and colleague Dr Konstantin Horvathy from accepting a prestigious post wanted for one of the brothers of the bell. The envelope contains photostats of photographs, names, and addresses of people who helped Dr Horvathy escape the oppressive Eastern European country of his birth. If the linguist refuses to back down, Patterson must threaten to make the documents public.

Glenn Ford was fifty-four when he played Patterson, but his uniform of suit and tie, short haircut and close shave makes him difficult to age. He could be ten years younger or older. Ford does a good job of sweating, lip trembling and generally looking like a man who has just realised he has founded his life on an oath of bad faith. He approaches Horvathy as a friend, initially trying to persuade him that he will be lonely if he moves to a new institution, then simply begging him to stay. Eventually he takes out the envelope and passes it to him. Horvathy is stunned by its contents. He asks, 'Do you realise what you are doing? These are men and women who will be shot. They will be taken to dungeons and to police stations, tortured, killed… Who are you?' Patterson cannot answer. By joining the Brotherhood of the Bell, the professor undertook a flight from freedom and long ago lost his authentic self.

Horvathy commits suicide. A brief shot shows him slumped half outside his bath, resembling Jacques-Louis David's post-death portrait of betrayed French revolutionary martyr

Jean-Paul Marat.[25] This is the cue for the next stage of the movie. Patterson finds he cannot live with the consequences of his actions. He turns whistle-blower and, like Caleb Williams and Mitch McDeere, comes under pursuit from ruthless forces. The difference is that Patterson is a seasoned member of the elite who, despite his denials, benefitted from the privilege of his affiliation. His mentor asks,

> 'Are you truly ignorant of what the Bell has done for you?... Because of the Bell, you have received every option, every fellowship, every post you ever wanted… you have never competed for one thing in twenty-two years since you first took the oath at sunrise.'

This is a world where the balance is firmly set in favour of the power elite. Patterson has a hard job persuading the authorities of the existence of the Brotherhood of the Bell. They are either in on the action or disbelieving. The district attorney scoffs at the concept of 'a white Anglo Saxon mafia of rich influential men'. Meanwhile, the brothers are busy. Patterson loses his job, his marriage and his father, who has a stress-related stroke and falls into a coma.

Oscar Slater must have experienced some of the same bewilderment as Caleb Willliams, Mitch McDeere and erstwhile brother of the bell Professor Andrew Patterson. Slater was a confident, widely travelled man used to negotiating the world.

---

25   www.britannica.com/topic/The-Death-of-Marat.

He had been drawn to Scotland by the Glasgow International Exhibition of 1901 and had previously helped run a couple of gaming clubs in New York. At the time of the murder, he was planning to return to the United States to establish a new club in San Francisco.

Initially, Slater was sure that he could prove his innocence. He had an alibi for the night of Miss Gilchrist's murder[26] and had pawned the diamond brooch days before the crime took place.[27] He was also not a good fit for the description of the man seen leaving Miss Gilchrist's flat.

Oscar Slater returned voluntarily to Glasgow from New York, against the advice of his American lawyer. It was a big mistake. After a police identification parade that put him in line with nine police officers and two railway men, Slater was remanded in jail and then placed on trial. He wrote to a friend, 'the police is trying hard to make a frame up for me... every man is able to get put in such an affair and being innocent'.[28]

The trial was overseen by a bastion of respectability, Lord Guthrie, teetotaller, legal advisor to the Free Church of Scotland

---

26 Oscar Slater was initially mistaken about the date of Miss Gilchrist's murder. He thought it occurred on 22 December, whereas it happened a day earlier on the 21st. Slater had alibis for both nights, but his alibi for the correct night was not presented at the trial.

27 Detective Inspector John Ord, who was in charge of the case, knew the pawn ticket for the brooch predated Miss Gilchrist's murder before he phoned New York police to request Slater's arrest and sent officers across the Atlantic to accompany Slater back to Glasgow. Indeed, news that the 'clue' was irrelevant was published in the *Glasgow Citizen* newspaper on 28 December 1908, making it public knowledge early in proceedings.

28 Jack House, *Square Mile of Murder, Horrific Glasgow Killings* (Black & White Publishing, 1961) p.148.

and President of the Boys Brigade.[29] The evidence against Slater was flimsy but much was made much of his alleged moral degeneracy. Lord Guthrie stated in his summing up to the jury, 'He has maintained himself by the ruin of men and on the ruin of women, living his life in a way for many years past that many blackguards would scorn to live.' The jury followed the judge's direction and found Slater guilty. Oscar Slater was sentenced to death. His execution was scheduled to take place on 27 May 1909. On 25 May, after a public petition, the sentence was commuted to life imprisonment.

The Trial of Oscar Slater by William Roughead, published a year later in 1910, paid meticulous attention to the weakness of the conviction. In 1912, Arthur Conan Doyle published a pamphlet, *The Case of Oscar Slater*, which made a convincing argument for Slater's innocence. In 1914, police detective John Trench, who insisted on evidence of Slater's innocence, was sacked after a 'Secret Inquiry' into the trial found the conviction safe.[30] It was not until 1928, after nineteen years in

---

29 Ben Braber, 'The Trial of Oscar Slater (1909) and Anti-Jewish Prejudices in Edwardian Glasgow', *History* Vol. 88, No. 2 (290) (April 2003).

30 Detective Trench's conscience would not allow him to let Oscar Slater moulder in jail for a crime he did not commit. In 1914, after various attempts to convince his superiors of the problematic nature of the conviction, Trench approached Glasgow solicitor David Cook with the story. Sharing police evidence with an outside party was a breach of police regulations and Trench was dismissed with dishonour. Trench and Cook were later tried for resetting jewellery. The case was thrown out of court, amidst applause from spectators, and reflected badly on the probity of the Glasgow police. In 1999 a commemorative plaque dedicated to Trench was unveiled in Glasgow Police Museum by Chief Constable Sir John Orr, but the dishonourable aspect of his dismissal has never been officially rescinded. Trench's entry on the Glasgow Police Museum website records his breaking of regulations and subsequent dismiss-

prison and a sustained campaign involving Sir Arthur Conan Doyle,[31] that Oscar Slater was released. Rumours about who the real killer might have been still circulate. Some involving conspiracy theories about 'respectable' members of Scottish society at the time. What is certain is that antisemitism and Slater's outsider status as a foreigner, whose income came from uncertain sources, were central to his conviction.

Oscar Slater's troubles did not end with his release. He and his wife, a Scottish woman of German extraction, were designated enemy aliens and interned for a period during World War Two. His extended family, including his two sisters, were murdered in the Holocaust.

Persecution in crime fiction pulses with excitement, danger and near misses. Mitch McDeere outwits his enemies and escapes with a fortune. Brother of the bell Professor Patterson finds an ally who will help him detonate the brotherhood's arsenal of privilege. Caleb Williams's fate is more complex. His tale has two endings.[32] The best-known version may have been

---

al. It makes no mention of his previous attempts to draw the miscarriage of justice to official attention, or of the fact that he was right in his assertions. www.policemuseum.org.uk/personalities/honours-and-awards/awards/detective-lieutenant-john-trench/

31   In later years Conan Doyle was bitter towards Slater, who he felt had not been grateful enough for the writer's contribution towards his release. He considered that Slater (who received £6,000 compensation) should repay the £1,000 Conan Doyle had contributed towards his defence. Slater refused. Doyle branded him 'the most ungrateful as well as the most foolish person whom I have ever known'.

32   D. Gilbert Dumas, 'Things as They Were: The Original Ending of Caleb Williams', *Studies in English Literature, 1500–1900, Vol. 6, No. 3, Restoration and Eighteenth Century* (Summer, 1966), pp.575–97 (Rice University).

constructed in response to ongoing persecution of writers and radicals.[33] In it, Squire Falkland confesses to murdering Tyrrel and dies shortly afterwards. A chastened Caleb recognises that his master was a good man brought down by society and blames himself for Falkland's death.

The original ending is less conciliatory. Poor Caleb is sent to jail by an unjust magistrate and loses his mind. His final words recall those of Winston Smith, the defeated antihero of George Orwell's *Nineteen Eighty-Four*:[34] 'it was all right, everything was all right, the struggle was finished. He had won the victory over himself. He loved Big Brother.' Caleb also concludes that the individual is helpless in the face of ruthless authority. Madness and passivity is the only sane response:

> True happiness lies in being like a stone – Nobody can complain of me – all day long I do nothing – I am a stone – a gravestone! an obelisk to tell you, There lies what was once a man!

I have made much of the role of respectability in miscarriages of justice. It represents power, prejudice, and a desire to

---

[33] Godwin was a courageous writer, political thinker and activist. *Caleb Williams* was first published in 1794, during a period of extended Treason Trials designed to crush radical opposition to government. Godwin was active in radical circles and knew many of the people on trial. In the same year he wrote a political pamphlet, *Cursory Strictures on the Charge delivered by Lord Chief Justice Eyre to the Grand Jury*, which attacked the case for treason against the leaders of the London Corresponding Society and the Society for Constitutional Information.

[34] George Orwell, *Nineteen Eighty-Four* (1949).

maintain propriety, or reassure a wealthy elite, which can result in rushed and unjust convictions. Recent events have intensified my impatience with the concept of respectability.

In the middle of writing this chapter, around nine o'clock at night, the bell to my flat rang unexpectedly and a friend came up to break the news that one of our friends and neighbours, a woman who lives alone, had been found dead. It took me a moment to realise that the cause of her death was not a sudden stroke, heart attack or aneurism, but violence.

I sat down on the top step of the landing, not quite able to process what he was telling me.

'What? She was murdered?'

My friend shook his head. 'No, someone killed her.'

The word 'murder' was too horrible to accept, the sudden reality of it too strange.

It has taken me some time to return to Oscar Slater and the murder of Miss Gilchrist. Miss Gilchrist's flat was a few doors away from where our friend lived. From my bedroom window I can see the six-foot wicker heart a group of people made and strung with flowers and solar lights in the days immediately after the police moved out. There is still a shrine of flowers and candles on the corner of our street. A laminated poster with a smiling photo is attached to the railings opposite my building.

I have been wondering how the occupants of our street felt back in 1908, when they heard of Miss Gilchrist's violent death. I imagine they felt as the current community do. Shocked, upset, angry, frightened, sad, disbelieving... Perhaps some of them stood in the street and cried, the way I have seen people cry recently. Talk of respectability is a sham. It is not respectability that is outraged by our friend's murder, it is all of us. Her friends and the community she was an active part of, and will continue to be part of, beyond death.

The false conviction of Oscar Slater was also a tragedy for Miss Gilchrist and her neighbours. I do not want to call it 'things as they are'. Godwin reflects the world with more clarity than novels where wronged heroes are triumphant. But crime fiction is not fixed. There is room for novels that remind us the world is a harsh place, and we must work hard if we wish it to be otherwise. And there is a need too for books that acknowledge danger while offering us some escape, however unrealistic. Novels where those who are assaulted overwhelm their attackers and live on to further adventures, respectable and otherwise.

Setting Out Your Stall

Carole Johnstone

I went to my very first FantasyCon way back in 2008. I had a grand total of two writing credits to my name: a very short story called 'The Morning After', which had been published in *Black Static* #3, and a flash piece that was to appear in an anthology being launched at FCon. I felt like an imposter even before I ended up sitting next to a well-known author at the launch itself. He was incredibly kind and gave me a lot of advice that I still use to this day. However, he said one thing in particular which – at the time – I completely disagreed with. He said that as much as he loved being a writer, he would never write outside of the genres he chose. In other words, if his books were no longer selling and his agent or publisher asked him to consider writing, for example, a commercial thriller, he wouldn't do it. He absolutely could, he assured me, but that was beside the point. He didn't want that to be part of his oeuvre, nor did he want to become a 'writer for hire': creating novels whose primary focus was only their commerciality, their marketability. Because – stop me if you've heard this before – writers write for the love of it, the art of it, and publishers publish only for the profitability.

Back then, that felt a little smug, and perhaps simplistic. And, if I'm honest, quite easy for someone who I considered already successful to say. For me, writing for writing's sake – to be able to write anything at all and have it published – had always been my greatest goal. For over twenty years, I'd worked in cancer services in the NHS. It was a physically and emotionally draining job, and any writing always took a back seat. I would write during holidays and at weekends, very occasionally in the evenings. And for twenty years I never came close to being able to write enough – or earn enough – to become a full-time writer.

In a Google search of 'How many writers have…', the predicate 'day jobs' comes just after 'killed themselves' and 'become billionaires'. Not incredibly scientific, particularly when the first is almost certainly statistically likeliest, but you get my point. For most writers, the average annual income is £10,500. Not exactly a liveable wage. All I have ever wanted to be is a full-time writer, that's probably true of most writers. But when I realised I was never going to get there by writing short stories and novellas, nor was I ever going to be able to complete a novel while doing the job that I did, I knew I had to make a choice. That's not true of everyone; plenty of writers can and do write novels alongside their day jobs all the time, but I was never going to be one of them. I was lucky and had savings enough that I could take an extended break from work, and it was then that I wrote my debut novel, *Mirrorland*. It was also,

I suppose, a way of cosplaying being a full-time writer without committing to it entirely. I loved it. Wrote and edited the book within six months, and then started the tortuous process of finding an agent.

I was incredibly fortunate in that after signing to my agent, *Mirrorland* sold quickly. My biggest stroke of luck was that NBC Universal optioned the TV rights before any publisher had bought the book, and that triggered two simultaneous auctions in the UK and the US around the London Book Fair in 2019. In the end, it sold to Simon & Schuster and Harper-Collins, and to fourteen other territories in translation rights. I made the front page of *The Bookseller*. Brilliant, I thought, I've done it. I've made it. I resigned immediately.

Over the following two years, I came back down to earth with a resounding bump. *Mirrorland* was chosen as a lead title for both publishers, with the marketing and publicity budgets that come with that. Publication was pushed back to 2021 to create a buzz. A US book tour was organised. And then Covid-19 struck. All my in-person events were cancelled. Bookshops remained closed on launch day. All that noise got very quiet. I started to fear that I hadn't actually made it after all.

Now, that's just the nature of writing, of course. There are never any guarantees except abject uncertainty. You have no idea if the next book is going to net you a six-figure advance or absolutely nothing at all. You have no idea if it will become a *Sunday Times* and *New York Times* bestseller, or vanish without a trace. And all the while, everyone will tell you – from writers to agents to editors and publishers – that the debut is king.

That here is your one chance to make it. And it is true that at the book fairs, it is invariably the big debut deals that make the headlines. And it's also true that it does often feel that writing is an all-or-nothing gig. That big success or big failure are the only possible outcomes. And it's your debut that will determine which.

But while it's true that you're never guaranteed a guarantee, and there's nothing sure about a sure thing, there's still plenty you can do to give yourself – and your books – the best possible chance. Before I sat down and wrote *Mirrorland*, I spent a long, long time deciding what to write. I don't mean what story, but what *type* of story. I had, by 2018, written and had published over fifty short stories and novellas. All were genre fiction. I'd initially started writing horror and sci-fi because I loved Stephen King. In particular, I loved his short stories. In fact, all my early published works read like King fanfic until I found a voice of my own. Genre fiction, too, was just about the only type of short fiction you could get widely published. Magazines like *Black Static, Interzone, Cemetery Dance*, and *Clarkesworld* allowed open subs, while indie publishers edited multi-author anthologies all the time. And so that's what I wrote. For years. I always assumed that when I came to write a novel, I would write a genre novel too. I remember buying the *Writers' & Artists' Yearbook* so that I could compile a list of potential agents to sub to, and making the alarming discovery that at the end of most agency entries was the same line: 'no genre or children's fiction'. Why? I suppose traditionally, there has always been a literary snobbery around genre fiction. And while both horror and sci-fi might have been popular in TV and film media, at the time that hadn't translated much to fiction. Publishers weren't interested; ergo, neither were agents. This stopped me in my tracks a bit, because while some agents did accept genre submissions, choosing something that had a lesser chance of attracting interest in an already competitive arena seemed like choosing to give myself a big handicap before I'd even begun. Within the book publishing industry, legend has it that the odds of a writer getting a novel pro-published is between one and two per cent, and the odds of getting an agent less than one. Logically, I thought, why make that even harder for myself?

So, I sat down, and I thought about it. I thought back to that author at FantasyCon. I remembered how much I'd disagreed with his very fixed views on selling out: on always being the kind of writer that stays true to herself, mortgage and fame be damned. At the same time, I looked at how what I liked to read had changed over the years, while what I wrote had not. I was, in fact, reading very little horror in my thirties; often, I found myself disappointed by new novels: they were derivative, predictable, plodding. My consumption of sci-fi had fallen off a lot as well; I began finding much of it impenetrable and ultimately unsatisfying. I had switched from reading nothing but men to reading predominantly women. And I was reading more widely, too: in addition to genre, I was reading crime and psychological thrillers, literary, romance, historical, fantasy, even YA. I reasoned that if I loved to read across a spectrum of different kinds of fiction, then surely I could write outside of my usual kinds of fiction too.

SETTING OUT YOUR STALL

I decided to look at the question of *what* from a purely logical standpoint. In my first life I was a scientist, a physicist, so I decided to view it like a vector equation. Cause and effect. What would give me the best chance at succeeding? What could I stand to write and (potentially) keep writing? A very dear and brilliant writer friend of mine once told me to write as often as I could and in as many styles and voices as I could, so that when it was time to set out my stall, I could be as well informed as possible before making my choice. She said – and I've come to see that she was exactly right – that the most critical thing about your debut novel is *what* kind of novel it is. Setting out your stall is vitally important because what you write first will become what you are. It will become what is expected from you going forward. So much of publishing is shorthand, is putting writers into boxes or stables; it isn't fair, but it will happen. To your agent and your publishers and your readers you are a horror writer, or a thriller writer, or a sci-fi writer, etc. That is you. That is what will immediately and always be associated with you.

If you're lucky enough to write in a genre that is either currently on trend (romantasy) or constantly on trend (crime fiction), then that dilemma is never really yours. If, however, what you write is either niche or has fallen out of favour, it will inevitably be a hard sell – both to publishers and readers – and you will inevitably be faced with a choice. You could carry on and perhaps manage to find a publisher and readership, but unless your kind of novel ever does become popular, yours will always be an uphill struggle.

Of course, one way around a not entirely successful debut, or a desire *not* to be put in a box or stable, is to choose another pen name and write a different kind of book. In this vein, you could technically debut as many times as you liked, although I doubt many agents would recommend it. Obviously, there's a balance to be had between sticking rigidly to your guns and shooting indiscriminately until something hits the target. But you can never lose sight of the brutal truth that you *are* a commodity, you will always be a commodity. And no one likes to buy one thing and end up with something completely different, publishers included. It takes a long time to write and edit a novel; under contract, most publishers expect a writer to publish once a year, at most once every two years. That doesn't give you a lot of spare time to branch out or be more than one kind of writer. Building a brand is as important if not more important than making a splash. Finding a loyal readership is like striking gold, and you must be prepared to give some of that loyalty back.

For my part, I scoured the bestseller lists and researched market trends. I looked at what kinds of stories agents were most interested in. I also took a much more forensic look at what I liked to write. I always thought I wrote horror and sci-fi, because that's what my stories were pitched and marketed as. I don't make a habit of reading reviews (and if any part of this essay should be taken as advice, that's probably the best: never read the reviews). However, in the name of research, I chose a few of my more successful published stories and googled them. Good reviews were helpful, but the bad ones were eye-opening.

For example, I'd written a sci-fi novelette called *Skinner Box* for Tor Macmillan in the US. This was the elevator pitch: 'A disturbing science fiction story about a seemingly routine scientific mission to Jupiter that is threatened by the interpersonal relationships of its crew.' Sex and domestic violence were pivotal to the plot (as was AI, nano technology, and the singularity), but the former led to many scathing gripes about my demeaning sci-fi and turning it into soap opera. I was even, for the first time in my life, labelled an 'authoress' for the transgression. Around the same time, I'd also written a serial killer short called 'Just (/'dʒʌst/)', for a UK horror anthology, and this story was subsequently run down in many reviews for being too crime and not enough horror.

I suppose, if nothing else, these examples show how important labelling can be to readers. And how rigidly, as a writer, you're often expected to stick to yours. But what those reviews showed me most of all was something that I'd never been able to see for myself. To me, *Skinner Box* had been a sci-fi story, and 'Just' a horror story, and that was it. But what they were really about was people. About the terrible and amazing things that people are capable of when put into extreme situations. About good and bad relationships; good and bad choices; bravery and depravity and everything in between. For me, people have always been the most fascinating and bottomless pit of inspiration.

I realised that I loved Stephen King not because he wrote horror or sci-fi, but because he knew how to write about people. I love how he writes about people. And that's how I try to write about people. Once you work out what the common themes underpinning your work are – and that's only one example of mine – it becomes easy to write almost any kind of fiction at all. A lot of the time, I think writers write what they do because that's what they've always written, but who of us is the same person we were ten or twenty years ago? I know I'm not. We're constantly re-evaluating and changing so many aspects of our lives as we live them, so why not this? At the very least, we owe it to ourselves and our career to keep checking if what we're writing is what we want – or perhaps need – to be writing.

In the end, I decided to write a psychological thriller because it was a publishing trend that was fairly steady. Not quite at crime fiction levels, but I preferred reading standalone stories to detective series or police procedurals, so it felt more doable. The audience is predominantly women, and it's an incredibly broad church; there are almost endless possibilities, thus good potential longevity. And so, feeling very pleased with myself and my decision, I started writing *Mirrorland*. But an unexpected thing happened when I did. Something that made me look at what that writer at FantasyCon had said in an entirely different light.

Mirrorland is set in a very creepy old house in Leith, and is basically about a woman trying to find out what's happened to her missing estranged sister, while being forced to confront their strange and terrifying childhood. *Mirrorland* is the imaginary world that they created under the house as kids, and initially wasn't intended to be a major part of the plot at all (or the title!). But the more into the story I got, the more it took on a life of its own, without me even noticing. The final book ended up being a third psychological thriller, a third gothic horror, and a third supernatural mystery. My follow-up novel, *The Blackhouse*, set on a fictional island off the coast of the Outer Hebrides, started out as a murder mystery, and quickly became part crime thriller and part gothic suspense, with a side helping of Norse mythology and reincarnation. My subconscious had finally recognised what my conscious and logical brain could not – that the perfect home for me was cross-genre fiction.

I tell people that I write gothic thrillers because that's what my books are marketed as, and publishers don't want to spend money on promotion only for you to turn around and call it something completely different. But my novels are a lot of other things too: horror, crime, suspense, murder-mystery, spicy romance, and there is *always* a speculative element, be it supernatural, spiritual, fantasy, or futuristic. This is undoubtedly because at my heart I will always be a genre writer. And it's impossible to entirely leave behind what you are. What your themes are. Your strengths. Your passions. Which is probably what that FantasyCon writer meant all along. That no matter what type of book you want to write, no matter how carefully you plan to set out your stall, you will always end up being the writer that you are.

But let me tell you, if my agent or editor were to turn around now and say, 'Will you write an *xyz* novel?' I would still most likely say yes. I'd just try to write it my way. Because, for me – and I can't see this ever changing – the act of writing, the privilege of being able to write, far outweighs any ideals I have of oeuvre or legacy. I would rather be writing *any* fiction full-time than working at a safe job I hate and writing whatever I feel like only in my spare time. I appreciate that this is not the case for everyone, nor should it be. Publishing can often feel like a great big mouth that's always hungry for new and now, but if you're savvy, if you cultivate your own voice, your own brand, and your own choices, it can – and will – still have room for you. With a bit of luck, over and over and over again. Until you realise that what you choose to write and what you love to write are one and the same thing. And both pay the mortgage.

The Mirrored Room

Saima Mir

Stories are the most powerful things on earth. They change people from the inside, and they do it without the reader realising what's happening.

I have always read to be entertained and to find a connection, to know that I'm not alone in the way I feel. When I write, my primary hope is similar: that I will take the reader on a journey, at the end of which they will be sad to have left the world and characters that I have created but I also want them to feel a connection.

My chosen genre, that of crime fiction, often acts as an arena for the anxieties of society and of individuals.

An arena is defined as a level area surrounded by seating in which sports, entertainment and other public events are held, and also a place, or scene of activity, or debate. In my work, this often centres around faith, race, community and loyalty. Crime fiction is all about entertainment, conflict, and activity, but it can also be about debate.

This was something that became evident as my debut novel, *The Khan*, hit the bookshelves in 2021. *The Khan* is set in a fictional northern town, and tells the story of Jia Khan, the reluctant daughter of a criminal kingpin. It went on to become a *Times* bestseller, a *Sunday Times* Book of the Year, and was hailed as 'genre-busting' by critics.

The very things that made it a bestseller are also what kept the manuscript hidden away on my computer for seven years prior to this. No one seemed interested in its themes, and my agent at the time couldn't sell it. As the seasons passed, and I became a mother to three boys, I gave up on the idea of it ever seeing the light of day. That was until an article I'd written for *The Guardian* went viral. Things sped up after that, and I found myself with a new agent, a book deal, and an editor.

In the time it took for the book to go from acquisitions to bookshelves, I matured as a writer, and George Floyd was killed. The murder of the African American man by police officers in the US had a ripple effect across the world: it was as if white society began seeing itself through the lens of people of colour for the first time. Books by Black women topped the bestseller lists, and the landscape that was publishing landscape changed: editors sought out manuscripts from global majority authors, initiatives were developed by publishers to enhance the diversity of their employees. It was against this backdrop that I made my literary debut.

I was born to a Pakistani couple who had moved to London in the 1970s. When I was two years old, they relocated to Bradford in West Yorkshire, where my grandfather was already settled. It was here that I was raised, attended university, and started my career as a journalist. The intersection of being

British, Pakistani, female and northern informed my world view. Collectively these things made me an outlier to success, but they also gave me a unique perspective on the world, and it was this that I used to form the foundations of the book that became *The Khan*.

As a reporter, with a background in news, I'm trained to write the facts about a place, people, and alleged incidents, within the constraints set out by media law. I am under obligation to report the truth about society as honestly as I can.

As a writer of fiction, the only constraints are the ones I create, but when tapping into my own race, religion and heritage I feel a personal obligation to spin my yarn in such a way as to expose the truth. This comes from growing up in a time when I saw communities to which I belonged misrepresented, maligned and viewed with very real fear.

After 9/11 and then 7/7, there was a shift in the way Muslims were seen and portrayed in the media. There was interest in who we were, how we lived, and what we believed, that was steeped in Islamophobia. The stories that were reported about us fed into the narrative of 'the other'. In order for the War on Terror to be justified, all Muslims had to be villainised. Countless stories were told about honour killings, grooming, about Muslim women needing rescuing from hijab, and from their families. Cities like Bradford and Birmingham were portrayed as ghettos, where people of Pakistani heritage refused to integrate, educate or take part in British society.

As a journalist for the BBC, I knew how hard it was to counter that narrative. Finding a story, setting it up, encouraging people to talk, and then getting an editor to agree to give it two minutes of airtime, was an uphill battle, and maybe audiences weren't ready to have their world view challenged. I started to lose hope, and the profession I'd chosen, one that I believed had the power to bring great change, began to strike me as weak.

I turned to fiction as a way of working through my ideas. Specifically, crime fiction became one of the vehicles through which I was able to introduce readers to the world of British Pakistani women. Having worked in news for twenty years, I had started to see the apathy that comes with being told facts repeatedly, the way that people become immune to the struggles of others, and how this can lead to divisions within society.

Growing up, the only place I could find books that told stories about people of colour was a tiny shop called Shared Earth, behind the Arndale Mall, in my home city. I read everything I could find by Maya Angelou, and Malcolm X, but I also read things like *Anne of Green Gables* and *Little Women*. These stories were about lives completely different to mine, but they helped me understand people who walked in shoes other than mine. Stories that give a glimpse of other worlds and lives help readers build empathy. Fiction creates a new world where we are free to explore our thoughts, our fears and our concerns.

As a writer of fiction, I found myself free to tell the version of the story that felt true to me, to tell the lie that exposed the truth.

Storytelling offers a wonderful place to examine society, where a writer gets to ask questions like 'What if?' In the case of *The Khan*, it began with 'What if Michael Corleone from *The Godfather* was a British Pakistani woman living in the north of England?' and went on to examine things like 'Why do British Muslims live the way they do? And are Muslim women really all oppressed?'

Crime writing allows us to pose questions safely, and although countless people may be shot, knifed and murdered in horrifying ways, no actual damage is inflicted in the real world. But there is another aspect to crime writing, one which comes with the privilege of being a storyteller, and that is having the freedom to bring the thoughts that torture us as individuals out into the light and give readers access to us in a way that is psychologically safe.

The human condition requires that the characteristics and events of our lives, the things that make us who we are, are seen and heard, that the pain we experience is looked on by someone else and validated, that the varied reasons for our right and wrong choices are understood, that we have a chance to make plain why we are the way we are, and what has been done to us. *The Khan* was a crucible into which I poured my anxieties about family, loyalty and community, along with race, religion, heritage, gender. The molten themes were then shaped into a story, told through the lens of a woman who shared my background, and had faced similar questions to the ones I had asked.

The protagonist of the story is a Muslim woman named Jia Khan. With her faith comes accusations from different parts of society, from within her community, and from outside. These experiences have shaped her and affected her in numerous ways. They colour everything in her life, from her dress to her relationships and career. Creating a character with these experiences, with whom readers could also empathise, was important to me. Finding ways to relate to someone, even though they come from a different background, race or religion, makes us less likely to fear them.

I tell stories to show people that we don't need to fear each other. In the case of *The Khan*, the fears of the characters are based on their experiences. They haven't separated themselves from each other or wider society because of a dislike of it, but because of grief, and that grief has turned to anger. Their criminality doesn't come from being born bad, but from an attempt to survive. While they are gangsters, my hope is that we still see the humanity in them, because it is only by connecting with each other that we make sure the patterns are not repeated.

I drew on my own experiences while writing, but it was only after the manuscript was complete, published and out in the world that I came to see what its true value was. A value that became even more apparent to me as I met and spoke with readers and fans of the novel at literature festivals across the country.

As a cub reporter at the *Telegraph & Argus* in Bradford, I'd often cover late shifts. This was my first job in journalism. The shift which ran from 3 p.m. to 11 p.m. involved making regular calls to the police and fire lines, following up leads, and developing contacts who knew what was really going on in the region.

I used to finish up what needed to be done, and head towards a café at the edge of the city centre, close to The

Alhambra Theatre, called Café Lahore. It was filled with young British Asians, looking for a place to hang out, chat and socialise. The walls were covered in images from classic cinema, both Hollywood and vintage Bollywood. The menu was a mix of karahis and grills, followed by school dinner puddings, a reflection of our second- and third-generation upbringing. I'd take my personal phone, my work mobile, and my notebook, which was covered in shorthand scrawl. I'd have dinner there and shoot the breeze with old friends and contacts, and make new acquaintances. It was here that the seed of *The Khan* was planted. This world that was never written about, but where I spent so much of my time.

As a journalist, I covered a variety of stories, and was given a glimpse into the lives of a cross-section of people. I was often sent to the reception desk of the smoked-glass building by the news editor, to meet someone who had walked in, and had asked to speak to a journalist. I remember one man who relayed a story to me, about a shady but powerful group of men who ran the city. Short and smelling of booze, he had greying hair and a face covered with lines and crevices. He was passionate about his tale, and convinced of its truth, but there was no evidence to back up his claims and he was obviously inebriated. Urban myths like this came fast and frequently during my career, and they watered the story's seeds in my head.

Court reporting, inquests, investigative pieces, were all good grounding for developing story ideas and characters: the scent of various courthouses, the sun shining on the street where a heinous crime has been committed, the broken look in the eyes of an accused. These things all stayed with me, like a box of textile cuttings, ready to be called up when I sat down to stitch *The Khan* together.

I met all kinds of characters, and my position allowed me to ask them questions I would not otherwise have been afforded. One of the best things about being a journalist is the privilege of mixing with people at all levels within society. I loved the city where I grew up, but the media seemed to concentrate on its racial divide, problems and poverty. They couldn't see the hope, the joy, and the real reasons for what was going on. The fact that these were real people with dreams and ambitions was conveniently forgotten. I always felt the region was judged, maligned and undersold. Yes, there were problems, but there were reasons for them, and there were people who wanted things to change.

My love for the city and its inhabitants gave me a sense of obligation to them. I did not want to do the city a disservice, and I felt that naming the place in a gangland crime story would do just that. So, I removed the place name from my manuscript. Because *The Khan* was also a labour of love, and a love story to the region where I grew up. It was not a representation of all facets of every Muslim woman, or every British Pakistani family, but it was a story that I wanted to tell at a particular moment in time. I hoped it would open doors into a world not always encountered by white society, and would allow other women to step through with their own tales.

The representation of Muslim women I had found in crime novels was of them as victims of circumstance, and oppression, with no agency of their own. Women who needed rescuing, or who were trying to escape their culture. But I was surrounded by clever, beautiful and inspiring Muslim women, who fought hard for their freedoms and for their rights. I wanted to see them on the page and to introduce them to the world. This was easier said than done. In addition to overcoming the structural barriers that global majority writers face within publishing, there is the greater challenge of being brave enough to speak one's truth, when no one else seems interested.

We often hear that writers must find their voice. This requires courage because it involves making oneself vulnerable about craft, skill and talent. As a Muslim woman, it comes with added complexity of revealing personal aspects of one's life that white society doesn't necessarily know about, and that the society one is raised in may not want told.

The skill is in the nuance, and mixing enough of the truth with the lie, to spin a story that holds attention and creates empathy.

The challenges for me, in addition to overcoming the fear that writers have of not being good enough, were stripping myself of what I thought publishers and white readers wanted, and letting go of the burden of being the representative of all Muslim experience.

All any writer can do is tell one story at a time, and crime novels rarely show us the best of humanity, but what they do provide is nuance. *The Khan* is the story of one specific woman, with light and shade. She's a criminal, but she is also a daughter, a mother, and a friend. She struggles, she fights, and she makes mistakes, all of which I hope presents her as someone real. Stories hold a mirror to society. My hope is that my work becomes a small section of the mirrored room that the world needs to see itself clearly from all angles.

Spotlight on...
Agatha Christie

On Reading as Escape: All of Christie's Murderers, and Me

Jessie Greengrass

The first detective novel I ever read was Agatha Christie's *The Murder on the Links*. The second was *Lord Edgeware Dies* in the old Fontana edition with a white banner heading on its cover and, underneath, a picture of the back of a man's head – the curve of his ear, the dome of his skull; each thinning hair lovingly drawn and, between the neatly clipped nape and his brown wool collar, a stiletto dagger sticking out of his neck. Blood trickled in a spreading pattern, staining his jacket, and if you looked hard – which, transfixed, I did – you could see the light reflecting off its bright red beads. I found this image so awful that before I could read the book I had to re-cover it in brown paper, snipping the paper to size and then folding it and securing it with Sellotape, all while looking out of the corner of my half-closed eyes, trying not to see the awful picture. Then I wrote the title on the front in my best print. Only after that was done could I open the book and begin to read, and this was thirty years ago but I can still remember it: the small typeface and the yellowing pages; the shimmer of fear which settled like a heat haze, superimposed across the world for days. There was a comfort in knowing what I was afraid of, and in knowing my fear of it to be unfounded. I wasn't a vivacious caricaturist with a barbiturate addiction, and nor was I an aggressively rude aristocratic throwback with a wife who wanted a divorce. No one wanted to kill me. I was ten, and lived in a small town in Devon. The world Christie created, and which with a very few exceptions all her novels inhabited – an un-ageing version of rural Edwardian England, its grand houses and their attendant villages populated by retired colonels and kindly vicars, by minor gentry and spinsters and the occasional glittering outsider – was such an obvious fantasy that the crimes committed there never really felt as though they could touch me. No evening-dressed poisoners stalked the staircase of our house although I often thought, with a kind of comfortable terror, that I could feel one there. It was the opposite to real life, where fear was a thing that loomed from corners and from edges, shrinking and growing according to a metric which I didn't understand. I felt, reading *Lord Edgeware*, that I had managed a kind of escape – to slip sideways into a world of clues and fancy houses in which all bad things, all crimes, were self-contained. Chaos never spilt outwards, there. People were easily decoded, their characters determined by their position, which was fixed. When bad things happened they were not the result of the complicated and apparently intractable interplay between multifaceted individuals and their socio-economic statuses, but were black and white: one motive per murder and, once the murderer was caught, the whole thing done and dusted. Crime as a kind of canker: a single, discrete entity which, with the right skills, could be excised whole to leave everything else behind, untouched.

* * *

Agatha Mary Clarissa Christie was born in Torquay in 1890, the youngest of three children. Her family were wealthy, staunchly upper middle class – the kind of people who, idealised, would later populate her novels, although like her characters they were not without their intricacies: Christie's mother, Clara, had been sent at the age of nine to live with an aunt who had a seventeen-year-old stepson. This stepson, Fred, would be Christie's father – and it's hard not to see in this a trace of the kind of intricacies Christies loved: relational ambiguities; people who occupied more than one role.

Although Christie began writing in her late teens, she was thirty before her first novel, *The Mysterious Affair at Styles*, was published, which seems remarkable now because it appears to be so fully formed. Although published in 1920 it was written in 1916, while Christie was working as a volunteer nurse and training as an apothecary's assistant – the plot of *Styles* revolves, at least in part, around the specific ways that medicines behave when kept. The novel features many of the elements which would later go on to be Christie's staples. Emily Inglethorp, the wealthy owner of Styles Court, dies suddenly, unambiguously murdered: she has been poisoned with strychnine, and leaves behind her a much younger husband and two stepsons who have been living in expectation of inheriting Emily's fortune. There is a companion and a loyal servant. There is a wife who manages her husband. There is a missing will. There are constructed alibis and there are disguises. The crime, when its details emerge, is both simple and not simple: it hinges on a single idea but is constructed intricately, although never quite to the point where the complex becomes the rococo. It is Christie's supreme talent that she is able to gauge so exactly the difficulty of her puzzles. They must be hard enough that the reader never quite solves them, but not so hard that they feel that they couldn't have done, if only they had tried a little harder. This is the satisfaction of them. They are like those puzzles, made out of two interlinking pieces of wire that must be pulled apart: impossible, until you see how it's done; and then, afterwards, absolutely obvious. It is a formula which she would repeat over and over again for more than fifty years and across eighty books, combining and re-combining the same elements but never, quite, repeating herself.

* * *

The year of *Lord Edgeware* was 1992 and the awful, unstoppable trainwreck of my parents' marriage had entered a new phase. My dad was moving out, leaving our upside-down house with its cavernous ground floor which had once been a commercial garage and was now the studio that my mum no longer had the will nor the time to use. Instead, Dad was going to live in a flat between the back of the butcher's shop and the town car park. I was afraid of the butchers', which had pig carcasses hanging behind the counter and a thick smell which billowed out onto the street so that I had to hold my breath when I walked past. I was afraid of the car park, too. I wasn't afraid of the flat, quite, but it was cold and it felt empty, all edge and surface. In my memory it appears perpetually half-dark, as though it was always five o'clock on a grey afternoon, waiting for someone to turn on the first light. The town was perched on the edge of the moor and it wasn't really home, although I couldn't remember living anywhere else. I had been born in London and lived there until I was four, moving only because the first time my parents split up my dad went to stay with his parents, who had moved to Devon from Surrey some years previously. After a while my mum and I followed him. Hills surrounded us. There was the constant sound of water, of rivers and of rain, and my mum hated it, her chronic inability to settle made worse by the fact that for the whole eight years we were there she kept on working part-time in London, leaving at 4 a.m. on a Wednesday to get the bus up from Exeter in time for work, then coming home again at midnight on a Friday – and I wonder, now, how much of this failure to commit was intentional. She must have known the edifice of our lives would be prone to subsidence – and now it had come, and the only real mystery was that it had taken so long.

After my dad moved out, for the half of every week that Mum was away, I went to school and then afterwards stopped at the house to feed the cat. Then I went to Dad's flat, and sometimes he was there, sometimes he wasn't. At the weekend, when Mum came home, she brought with her a confusing intensity, like something normal re-drawn at one and a half times its real size. Dad came round often. He cooked in the kitchen. He took baths, and sometimes stayed the night. What they had achieved, it seemed, was not so much a separation as it was a reconfiguration: a way to make themselves unhappy in two places instead of one; and if the result of it wasn't the absolute worst year of my life, then it was certainly in the top five. I carried my book with me from place to place and before long I'd finished the half-shelf or so of Christie novels we had in the house, and then I started getting them out of the library, these ones the newer, updated Fontanas which had Christie's name at the top and the title at the bottom, the font large and slightly retro, a smaller, more allusive image in the middle; and I was proud of myself, having achieved at last the distinction of reading adult books, viz, ones where the author's name was given at least equal billing to the title. I spent as many hours as I could in that parallel world – a place which was apart; a kind of refuge. In that world, everything always came good. All problems were solved. The detective, arriving on the scene, untangled all the threads and put them right again. Guilt could be divined and justice, when it came, came as an inevitability. It burned very hot and very bright, and left everyone innocent unscorched.

* * *

As much as the years between the end of the First World War and the beginning of the second were years defined by trauma, they also constituted a period of enormous social upheaval, this combination resulting in an outpouring of literary achievement. These were the years of Joyce and Woolf; of T.S. Eliot; of Katherine Mansfield. E.M. Forster. D.H. Lawrence. These were also Christie's years – the golden age of detective fiction, with her at the centre of it, fuelling an apparently insatiable public appetite for murder. By the end of the 1930s Christie had developed all the characters who would recur through her following forty years of work. She had developed and set her form, which would remain virtually unchanged for the rest of her career, and she had completed both *The Murder of Roger Ackroyd* and *Murder on the Orient Express* – the two novels which have probably the strongest claim to be her masterpieces, the greatest examples of her skill and ingenuity. Christie's novels, though, unlike their literary counterparts, don't deal with the specifics of her time. Instead, they offer a confection – a fantasy. It's easy to believe that, because of this, they are in some way less rooted in their time. A fantasy, though, is always counter to a specific reality. The particular form Christie's novels took, and would continue to take until her death in 1976, was determined by the time in which she was writing. What she offers in *Styles* is an idealised version of pre-war life – not just its concrete details but its morality, rooted in rigid social hierarchies. She is remarkably loyal to this vision. Even when, later, details of modernity intrude – in *Third Girl* (1966) for example, which could easily be re-titled *Poirot Meets the Beatniks* – they do so as a kind of visitation from a realm which is fundamentally alien. 'These girls!' Poirot thinks, after his first encounter with Norma Restarick, 'Do they not even try to make something of themselves?' – but although the novel takes place in London flat shares and artists' studios it is rooted in the place which Norma has come from: the village of Long Basing, and her father's house, just off the main street, 'neither beautiful nor ugly… It still had smooth green lawns, plenty of flower beds, carefully planted areas of shrubs to display a certain landscape effect. A gardener was certainly employed.' The sense of nostalgia is palpable, but, as is often the case with Christie's later novels, the nostalgia presents itself as being less for a real moment in time than it is for a place which Christie herself has, in some way, imagined. Just as P.G. Wodehouse's universe was a fantasy of aristocratic life, so was Christie's an idealised rendering of the upper middle classes, circa 1920: a world of weekend house parties and of sleepy semi-rural community which Christie herself has created.

This sense Christie creates of a lost world or of a world besieged by the modern (think of Miss Marple regretting the housemaids of her youth, the deficit of suitably subservient young women inextricably linked, somehow, with the awful encroachment of the housing scheme) was as much a response to her time and experience as the work of any other writer of the 1920s, but which satisfied a different urge: not to reflect, but to retreat. It's tempting to see this as the lesser aim, but surely that depends on your metric. She isn't a literary writer, nor even, often, a very good one, although in her lighter novels, such as the Tommy and Tuppence sequence, she demonstrates a comic talent which is often overlooked. As a craftsperson, though, she is exemplary. More than any other writer I can think of, her books appear alchemical, their particular mixture of ingredients which, in someone else's hands, would remain leaden, but which in hers become transformed into something like a golden afternoon: a discrete unit of time, self-contained and elsewhere, offering nothing more complicated than enjoyment.

* * *

In the summer of 1994, my mum and I left Devon. Nominally we left my dad, too, although in reality my parents' relationship persisted in one form or another for the best part of another decade. We were going back to a London I had been born in but which I couldn't remember, beyond a few disconnected scraps: a red bucket on a paved yard and a slide with a man standing at the bottom of it; snapdragons growing beside a wall; crocuses underneath a tree. First, though, I was going to stay at my grandparents' house for the holidays. Mum put me on the bus to Ipswich and after that, for five weeks, all through the long, dusty days, I lay on a sun lounger in the garden and read detective stories. My grandmother had an almost complete set of Agatha Christie novels and at the end of the summer she gave them to me, so that when Mum picked me up at last they were waiting with me in boxes to come in the car as we drove back across East Anglia's agricultural flatlands, past Colchester and through Essex and then down at last on the new link road, in through the city's eastern industrial sprawl and towards our new house where, in my new bedroom, I unpacked the books onto my shelves. I still have them. They have become, as books can be, a kind of constancy: a place, however unreal, which is always available. I could go back there and find it waiting, entirely orderly: the same faces and the same plots; the same country houses and vicarages and villages. Many of them have spines which are cracked into near-illegibility. Some are held together with elastic bands. The pages have turned brown and, held in the hand, they feel like fragile things, or like the remnants of fragile things – eggshells or dried leaves; the delicate stuff a wasps' nest is made of. I can read their titles like a litany and there I am at once: a train carriage at Istanbul or a boat on the Nile. Bertram's Hotel. Styles, with its windows and its tennis court. Places in which good and evil can be pulled apart, carefully, and then presented back to us while we sit and smoke cigars. The incontrovertible truth. No lasting shadows; no shades of grey.

Now it is January 2024. Outside it is very grey. The world unravels. The news makes me cry. I try to bring my children up to be kind, but also to be sturdy. I try not to think about what things will be like, by the time they are at the age that I am now. Sometimes, in the evenings, tired and heavy, I go and stand in front of my shelf of Agatha Christie novels and pick one at random: *Sleeping Murder* or *Endless Night*. *The Mystery of the Blue Train*. *Peril at End House*. I read the first few pages of one, and then of another, but I feel as though I am trying to catch something which is just beyond my grasp. I wait for the moment when I will be engrossed, but it doesn't come.

* * *

Although it's true that *The Mysterious Affair at Styles* is notable as a debut for being in many ways as much an exemplar of Christie's style as any of her later books, it is also unusual in being rooted in a particular time. Poirot, as he first appears, is a refugee from a Belgium torn apart by war (250,000 Belgians fled to the UK during the First World War, the biggest influx of refugees in British history). Hastings is recuperating after being wounded on the Western Front. There is a palpable sense of loss – of a way of life that is limping towards its end. You can feel it in Styles Court, a house which drifts, surrounded by tennis courts and rose bushes, against its backdrop of war into a world of which it isn't quite a part. The house is an anachronism, and so are the people in it. They turn inwards, bolstering one another against the turning tide with parties and cocktails, afternoon tea on the lawn and a little light murder on the side.

This sense of Christie's characters as inhabiting discrete bubbles becomes less explicit as her novels become less centred on a particular time, but it remains deeply embedded in her plots – not, I think, as a quirk or as a contingency, but as an essential driver. It's a part of what makes them work. The country house is a locked room, its inhabitants isolated – disengaged from the world beyond the walls so that the pool of suspects remains small. Christie's other go-to setting, the English village, performs the same function. The people who live there are tied to one another, resolutely refusing to engage with that great blank beyond the parish bounds, although as the years go on this empty space becomes for Christie ever more haunted by the spectres of the new-build housing estate and the lipsticked shop girl. Hotels, too, provide a convenient limitation, as do boats and trains. While it is true these spaces are fundamentally wealthy ones, it isn't wealth which defines them for Christie, but class. We must take it for granted, if we are to fully inhabit Christie's world, that the people about whom she writes, by dint of being upper middle class, must also obviously be rational and decent, moral and sane; and so murder, when it happens to them, must happen for a reason. A chap doesn't just bludgeon another chap, but neither does he get bludgeoned. The dead are almost always framed as being, in some measure, culpable in what happens to them – by being awful people who delight in winding up those around them beyond endurance, perhaps, or by being cantankerous and frequently changing their wills; but also by being poor, or tarty, or arriviste. Or, as in the case of second victims, because having seen something suspicious they choose, rather than doing what any decent person would do and going to the police, to try their hand at blackmail – thereby proving themselves immediately and inherently dishonourable, and so exempt from our sympathy.

Far from being an accidental function of the times in which she is writing, Christie's reliance on class tropes is essential to the mechanics of her books. What she sells to us is the fantasy of a world in which right and wrong are clear-cut, but this fantasy is specifically centred on an idealised version of a lost England: one in which everyone knew their place and belonged there; or if they didn't belong there, it was because they were an intentional imposter. Her books are profoundly moral, which is not to say that they are virtuous, but only that their compass is unwavering. They are xenophobic (consider the character of Pilar in *Hercule Poirot's Christmas*: her foreignness is coded as both ruthless and inherently untrustworthy). They are also antisemitic – in *The Hollow* a character is described as 'a Whitechapel Jewess with dyed hair and a voice like a corncrake… a small woman with a thick nose, henna red and a disagreeable voice.' Any deviation from straightforward, upright Edwardian Englishness is suspect, particularly so in men, whose sexuality must be lustful but also constrained by specific codes of honour. In *Murder is Easy* the hero, slab-faced Luke Fitzwilliam, who sees a beautiful girl and is determined to win her, is contrasted with Mr Ellsworthy, who deals antiques and takes arty photographs and so is clearly and immediately recognisable as a suspect. The outsider functions in Christie's novels, as in all these examples, as a red herring: it is assumed that we will perceive them automatically as suspect, but in fact they are rarely if ever the actual murderer, being not central enough.

SPOTLIGHT ON... AGATHA CHRISTIE

After a while, if you've read a lot of them, it becomes possible to guess Christie's murderers not by figuring out the plot but by understanding how she ranks her characters. Her murderers mustn't be obvious. They can't be any one of these outsiders who would bring to her novels too much of a sense of the world beyond: their motives would be too complicated, and so the bubble would be pierced. They can't be anyone too obviously virtuous either. An Edwardian moral code persists through all Christie's novels. No real gentleman would ever murder someone, not so much because it would be wrong, as because it would be cowardly and dishonourable. Christie relies, for the construction of her books, on typecasting. Her characters are tropes, not because she couldn't make them otherwise, but because it's only through recognising these tropes that we know where to put our suspicions. It's part of the fun, or is intended to be. We recognise untrustworthiness of character in the same way that we recognise a smashed watch or a fragment of unburned paper in a grate: a clue, either real or faked.

It's fundamental, too, that her murderers are always a little less than they ought – that they should have a fatal character flaw. We have to believe that they aren't us, any more than the victims are. This is how Christie pulls off the trick of drawing us in but keeping us at a distance. We are invested in the plots, but not the characters. It's why they're never, really, very frightening: because we know that, within the narrow confines of these country houses, these rectories and cottages, the flame of justice burns hot but also very exactly. It would never burn us. On the few occasions where she oversteps these bounds – at the end of *Nemesis*, for example, and once again in *A Murder is Announced* – the result is novels, or at least parts of novels, which are both better and also less good. Both instances feel unintentional, as though the realities of grief have crept in by accident, all the more horrible for being so unexpected.

* * *

This is what I learned, those months of 1992 and '93 when I read pretty much nothing but Agatha Christie novels. I learned to distrust policemen and also men who wear the wrong shirts, especially if those men have spent time in South Africa. I learned that diamonds, unpolished, look exactly like pebbles, and any alibi revolving around a watch is automatically suspect. That at any given country house party at least fifty per cent of the guests will be other than they seem. That hats make improbably good disguises, but dying your hair with peroxide and wearing nylons will almost certainly get you killed, probably by strangulation. I learned that the perfect length for a novel is 180 pages. I learned who all the murderers are – and perhaps, if Christie's novels don't work for me in quite the same way as they used to, then it's only because of this. I think, more often that I would like to admit to, of a scene in the sitcom *Red Dwarf* in which a spaceship's AI begs to have all of Agatha Christie's novels wiped from his memory so that he can read them again, and I wonder if this is something I would go for, if I could – but I don't think so. They're too bound up with my life, and too central to my idea of myself as a reader. And as much as I find it hard to enjoy them in quite the same way as I did, I still love them. They are still, on their own terms, perfect – but perhaps this is what bothers me. Things change. I change. What Christie taught me, when I first read her, was the enormous power of books as a means of comfort and escape – and while I also believe in literature as a form of engagement with the world (to read and to write our fears seems, often, to be the only available act both of protest and of hope), I still believe that escapism is profoundly important. These are extraordinary times – as extraordinary, in their way, as those years when Christie began to write – and we have to live. It's good to step away, sometimes, into an easier version of the world.

Of course, there are contemporary detective novels which work according to different rules. Ian Rankin's books remain an absolute delight, but while never less than gripping they are also too complex, too morally ambiguous, too much about the world to offer quite the same sense of refuge. Many of the writers who have written more explicitly in Christie's mould – Ruth Rendell, say, or Colin Dexter – have also co-opted her flaws and, in Dexter's case, doubled down on them. The detective form is adaptable, though, particularly when played, as Christie did when at her best, at least partly for laughs. Of its contemporary incarnations, the best – the most fun; the most engrossing – appear on screen: *Glass Onion*, say, or *Only Murders in the Building*, both of which play, explicitly or implicitly, on Christie's tropes. Here, it's humour that insulates us from having to think too much. There is an embracing of their own absurdity which is rarely less than joyful – none of

Christie's heavy moral pronouncements but shades, instead, of Tommy and Tuppence, of Ariadne Oliver with her apples and her endlessly restyled hair, of *Why Didn't They Ask Evans*'s Bobby and Frankie. I would like to see the equivalent in print, and I'd do it myself, perhaps, except it's harder than it looks – and besides, I'd know who did it, then.

Often, books which are primarily designed to offer escape are derided, along with the people who read them – as though to want to escape is to demonstrate, necessarily, one's obvious inferiority, or one's failure to care appropriately about the world. This is, I think, a particularly mean form of contempt, as well as being a false equivalence. It isn't a case of either/or. A person can look for more than one thing in literature – can want both art and entertainment; can need, at different times, both to be challenged, and to be allowed a rest. This is the glory of the novel: that it can be so many things. It was something Christie seemed, intuitively, to understand. She saw that what her readers wanted wasn't necessarily the world reflected back at them, but to be let out of it, for a little while. To be able to find, at will, a single golden afternoon and the certainty, however fantastical, that everything will come good in the end. That those who deserve it will be punished and the rest of us will walk away, undamaged and free.

THE OPPORTUNITY

Despite all that's been said about the universal qualities of the genre, crime fiction can take many guises. A psychological thriller told from the point of view of the criminal, in the vein of Patricia Highsmith's Ripley novels, may seem to share little common ground with a cosy crime caper à la *Agatha Raisin*. Equally, a classic police procedural is a world away from an amateur sleuth in the Middle Ages.

The one constant is the act of transgression: the crime itself. These essays interrogate four different subgenres of the genre – historical crime, crime in translation, police procedural and the locked-room mystery – and the ways that they're crafted, in the hope of unveiling their *modus operandi.*

Making the Dead Dance: Historical Crime Fiction

Vaseem Khan

The Starting Point: A Love of History

I love history. It was my favourite subject in school and the one I found myself most eagerly looking forward to. History lessons were a bright spot in the curriculum, coming as they did directly after the ordeal of our weekly art class where every portrait I painted resembled a cross between the Elephant Man and Frankenstein's monster. I particularly loved tales of blood and violence, be they Henry VIII's unique approach to marital discord or gut-wrenching vignettes from the Somme.

And yet, so often, this school-taught history was dry, pressed into the pages of glossy textbooks, devoid of that vivifying spark that truly sets flesh on the bones of the past.

That all changed when I came across a novel called *Shōgun* by James Clavell.

Shōgun is a historical adventure, set in medieval Japan, narrating the tale of a shipwrecked English sailor, John Blackthorne, who finds himself in a discombobulating land of samurais, shoguns and a sensual, sophisticated culture unlike anything he has experienced. As Blackthorne navigates this alien place he finds himself reassessing his view of both the Japanese and his own countrymen.

The book inflamed my curiosity. Until then I'd known nothing about Japan or its history. I would later discover that Blackthorne was based on a real person, a man named William Adams, the first Englishman to reach Japan (in 1600) and who would later go on to become a 'western samurai' and a valued advisor to the then Shōgun – the 'emperor' of medieval Japan.

This, then, was my first lesson: namely that historical fiction can borrow liberally from historical fact and in so doing teach us about the past.

A second lesson follows logically. One of the reasons readers are passionate about the genre is because it can reveal new facets of a subject they may consider themselves familiar with.

For me this happened with the novel *Birdsong* by Sebastian Faulks.

Prior to reading the book (in my early twenties), I thought I pretty much knew all I needed to know about the First World War, imbibed from the school history lessons I mentioned above. But it wasn't until I read *Birdsong* that I found myself thrillingly invited to set foot in the trenches alongside ordinary soldiers, to live, vicariously, their terror, their courage, their hopelessness, their small moments of optimism and camaraderie. The book, written in punishing and often beautiful prose, left an indelible impression on me and revised my idea of what the First World

War had truly meant for millions of ordinary soldiers.

The lesson? If you aspire to write historical crime, read historical fiction – and lots of it.

Discovering *Your* Period

Today, I write historical *crime* fiction, and I can draw a direct line between books such as *Shōgun* and my Malabar House novels. Indeed, one of my principal characters is called Archie Blackfinch – a tribute to *Shōgun*'s John Blackthorne. Like Blackthorne, Blackfinch is an outsider, an Englishman working in post-colonial India, gradually coming to grips with an alien society.

The Malabar House novels are set in 1950s Bombay, and began with *Midnight at Malabar House*, which won the Crime Writers Association Historical Dagger in 2021, the world's premier prize for historical mystery fiction. The books were born of my desire to explore India just after Independence, a nation still reeling in the wake of Gandhi's assassination and the horrors of Partition when a million Indians died in communal riots. My lead character, the newly qualified Inspector Persis Wadia, India's first female police detective, is determined to prove herself in a man's world, but is banished to Bombay's smallest police station, the eponymous Malabar House, a place populated by rejects and misfits.

Persis must work with Archie Blackfinch – it's a difficult pairing. Persis has battled through India's Independence movement, while Archie, to most Indians, represents the Raj

– though he took no part in it himself, having only recently arrived in Bombay from the Metropolitan Police in London to help set up Bombay's first forensic science lab.

In *Midnight at Malabar House*, Persis and Archie are called upon to investigate the murder of a senior English diplomat in his Bombay mansion. The book follows their efforts against a backdrop of a turbulent Indian society finding its feet in the post-Independence era.

That book allowed me to finally express my nerdy love of history. It followed on from a series of five novels I wrote set in *modern* India, the Baby Ganesh series, about a middle-aged Indian policeman in Mumbai, forced into early retirement, and who continues to pursue cases as a private detective while grappling with the unusual problem of inheriting a baby elephant. The series began with *The Unexpected Inheritance of Inspector Chopra*, a book that reflects my own observations of India after I lived there for ten years in my twenties. The book went on to become a bestseller, translated into seventeen languages.

Having written five books in the series, I realised that I wanted to know where this India that I had witnessed had come from. Though India is an ancient culture, it is also true that her foundations were established shortly after the country gained Independence and in the wake of three hundred years of the British presence on the subcontinent.

So, in essence, it was my own desire to excavate the past, an itch that simply had to be scratched, that led me to dig into the historical archives, which in turn led me to writing the Malabar House novels.

***

As the series has progressed, I find myself delving deeper into questions that have long plagued me about that period in India.

In *Death of a Lesser God*, the fourth and latest in the series, an Englishman named James Whitby – born and raised in India – is convicted of murdering an Indian lawyer. With eleven days until Whitby is hanged, Persis and Archie are forced into a reinvestigation – Whitby claims he is innocent, the victim of a desire by the Indian government to make him pay for the sins of colonialism. The question this book asks is a simple one: *can post-colonial societies treat their former colonisers justly?*

The novel begins in Bombay, before the action moves to Calcutta, where a cold case might be linked to Whitby's alleged crime – that of the murder of an African American soldier just after the war.

This was something I knew nothing about until I uncovered it in the course of my research, namely, that 150,000 American soldiers came to Bengal during the Second World War to help stop the Japanese advance through Burma, and some 20,000 of them were African Americans. In Calcutta, these African American GIs crowded out the local bars, haggled in the brothels, and expressed themselves freely with the locals – who had never encountered Black men before.

Calcutta, of course, was the first colonial capital of British India, with the colossal Writers Building, in what was then known as Dalhousie Square, housing the monolithic bureaucracy needed to govern the subcontinent – 'writers' being the name for the army of East India Company clerks who populated the place, dressed in woollen suits in the searing tropical heat, mildewing in the annual monsoon, and dying, variously of dysentery, malaria, and drunkenness. Over time, the city became mired in the Independence movement, until, in 1911, fed up with the argumentative Bengalis, the British upped sticks and moved their base to Delhi. In *Death of a Lesser God*, I describe the city thus:

> Once a pestilential riverine swamp, infested by bamboo jungles where tigers roamed freely, snacking on unsuspecting locals, the city was, in part, an invention of the British, who'd purchased the rights to the local land and the villages that sat upon it. One of those villages had been Kalikata, from which it was said Calcutta took its name.

And this brings me to another reason why I am passionate about historical mystery fiction: the ability to not only entertain but to raise from the dead both places and people, to set the reader in the very midst of a bygone age... complete with savage samurais and ravenous tigers.

Golden Age Historical Crime

I recently went to the cinema to watch *A Haunting in Venice*, the latest in the trilogy of Agatha Christie adaptations directed by Kenneth Branagh whose portrayal of (arguably) Christie's most enduring creation, Hercule Poirot, bears very little in physical resemblance to the written character. The original Poirot is described as possessing an 'egg-shaped' head. We are also left with the distinct impression of prim, waxed moustaches. Branagh's hipster-esque facial hair takes poetic license with Christie's depiction – but all is fair when it comes to adaptations. After all, Tom Cruise played Lee Child's Jack Reacher, even though Reacher is blond, six and half feet tall, and as wide as a barn door. Tom Cruise may be a fine actor, but even he cannot physically morph into the character as Child had written him.

Not that any of this has had any impact on the popularity of the Branagh-directed series. Collectively, the trilogy has grossed over $600 million.

Whatever you might think of the series' critical merits, there is little doubt that the films have tapped into the lucrative worldwide resurgence in popularity of the Golden Age of crime – or detective – fiction. Agatha Christie has sold over a billion books. We are told that only God and Shakespeare have sold more – though there is little doubt that if she keeps going at her current rate, she may soon supplant both at the top of the publishing heap.

* * *

Why is the Golden Age so important to today's historical mystery writers?

The answer, for me, is embedded in the way that Golden Age mystery tropes continue to appeal to a broad base of readers, and the way that the Golden Age can encompass so much more than a narrow band of time between the 1920s and '30s.

Today, when we talk of contemporary Golden Age mystery fiction, what we mean is fiction where the sex, blood and swearing is left offstage, and the focus instead is given to character and puzzle – what I call 'the intellectual challenge' of a good crime novel.

It's the reason I chose to write in that mode with my Malabar House novels.

To offer another example, the second in that series, *The Dying Day*, is about a priceless 600-year-old copy of Dante's *The Divine Comedy* that goes missing from Bombay's Asiatic Society. As Persis and Archie search for the manuscript, they uncover a series of cryptic clues, written in verse, pointing to various destinations and artefacts within the city. Bodies begin to pile up, increasing the stakes.

The book is inspired by Dan Brown's *The Da Vinci Code*, given a Golden Age makeover. The puzzles – and their solutions – power the narrative, rather than the central murder. Moral conundrums also abound, another feature of the Golden Age novel.

Perhaps most importantly, the characters that feature in my novels – and many others by historical mystery writers using the Golden Age as a blueprint – evince something I call 'likeability'. Likeability does not mean being perfect. Think back to the likes of Poirot. An egomaniac, a fusspot, and an undeniably prickly customer. But it is these very quirks that endear him to us, that make us want to spend time with him, book after book.

The tropes and traditions of Golden Age crime continue to be employed by many writers across a fantastically varied range of stories. And, if the response of readers is anything to go by, this never-ending Golden Age will continue for a good while yet.

Breaking the Mould

It would be impossible to discuss historical crime fiction without mentioning *The Name of the Rose* by Umberto Eco. Not only did the book become one of the bestselling novels of all time, but it redefined the very idea of a crime novel and what the genre might aspire to. And that is because it is so much more than a crime story.

Eco's seminal novel follows a fourteenth-century Franciscan monk who arrives at a wealthy Italian abbey to investigate heresy and is subsequently called upon to solve seven deaths, each more bizarre than the last. The book presents not just a fiendishly clever murder mystery and a detailed window onto life in the Middle Ages, but also serves as a philosophical meditation on the nature and place of man in his world and religion in the life of that world. It is a touchstone for the 'erudite crime novel', comfortably bridging the (ofttimes artificial) divide between literary and crime fiction.

Books such as *The Name of the Rose* are very much a product of their authors. The number of writers who could have written such a novel is vanishingly small, bordering on zero. Eco was a celebrated Italian semiotician and Joyce scholar, a man who revelled in intellectual riddles, laboured in the pursuit of historical meaning, and delighted in wordplay. That he chose to combine these passions in a crime novel is a testament to his versatility and (one supposes) the allure of the genre.

Eco brings to life the Middle Ages in a way that leaves readers not only informed but informed in a way that challenges us, demanding that we modernise our thinking. No longer are we permitted to romanticise the era. Instead, we are treated to the harsh political realities of warring popes, heretical, predatory monks, and a refutation of the unity of religious and political thought.

I call this historical 'correctionism'.

One of the reasons I write my Malabar House novels is because of a sense of injustice. Britain and India were in a three-hundred-year relationship, one that was detrimental to Indians – though not entirely. By the time the British left, India was irrevocably changed. And yet, in the history education I received growing up here in the UK, the subject of the British time on the subcontinent was barely touched.

It was only after I lived for a decade in India that I became intrigued by the history of my heritage. The Malabar House books evolved out of a desire to showcase some of the things I had learned and that I wish I had been taught in school. I sprinkle such facts throughout the series, when they can be woven in without distracting from the narrative.

So, for instance, in *Midnight at Malabar House*, I mention the fact that two Indians were responsible for inventing the fingerprinting classification system that we still (largely) use today. The Indians in question, based in Bengal, were sidelined by history; the system they developed was named after their British supervisor and thus became known as the Henry Classification System, later exported to Scotland Yard.

In the third book in the series, *The Lost Man of Bombay* – about the death of a white man found frozen in a cave in the foothills of the Himalayas with only a notebook containing cryptic clues – I mention George Everest, the Welshman after whom Mount Everest is named. Yet Everest never went near the mountain, nor did he determine that it was the world's tallest peak. That effort was led by an Indian named Sikdar. Everest was a surveyor in India, a successful one. In order to honour him, the Royal Society decided to name the mountain after him (ignoring the various Indian names already attached to the peak).

Many factors can feed into the desire to write historical crime, but a wish to rectify the wrongs of history or shine a light on a topic of interest are two that might be familiar. And if such an effort can overlap with writing that breaks boundaries, so much the better.

Striking a Balance

What is the right balance to strike between the mystery and the historical elements in a historical crime novel? As writers who spend an inordinate degree of effort researching our chosen period, there is a tendency to want to shoehorn in as much as possible. Historical fiction lends itself to a certain degree of exposition, a larger and often lusher canvas. But the central requirement of any crime novel is to entertain. And that means the narrative must have forward momentum. It cannot become bogged down in unnecessary exhibitionism.

Having said this, historical fiction readers do tend to be more forgiving than readers of other genres, willing to allow authors a little breathing room. There is an understanding that recreating the past requires a certain expansiveness.

The acid test is to examine each chapter, each scene, each paragraph and make an honest judgement as to whether or not it is adding something tangible to the book: advancing the plot, developing a character, or setting the scene. I spend hours researching the period I write about. The desire to showcase more of that effort than would be good for my books is a siren song that can easily lure me onto the rocks.

Of course, this equation is governed, to a certain extent, by the demands of the subject matter, or by the extent of an author's readership.

C.J. Sansom's incredibly popular *Shardlake* novels have gradually increased in length from the four-hundred-page range for the first, *Dissolution*, to well over eight hundred for book seven, *Tombland*. Sansom has a large and committed following, readers who enjoy his detailed world-building and complex plotting. The books follow hunchbacked lawyer Matthew Shardlake as he navigates the political and religious intrigues of Henry VIII's Tudor England. The novels are peppered with mythical figures from history: Thomas Cromwell, Thomas Cranmer, and even a young Elizabeth I.

* * *

On the point about research: how much *is* too much?

One of my favourite books – and a direct inspiration for my Malabar House series – is *A Suitable Boy* by Vikram Seth. Firstly, as a purely literary endeavour it's an incredible achievement, one of the longest and most complex books in the English language (1,300 pages). More importantly, it captures a time in Indian history that is both important and not very well explored in fiction. We have plenty of stories about the Raj, but very few about what came immediately after. *A Suitable Boy* captures both the turbulent politics of the time, but also the society in which these great events were taking place, in granular and immersive detail.

Seth spent years locking himself away, basically ignoring his friends and family. The book became an absolute obsession – and you can see this on the page. Seth committed to getting everything right. For instance, he spent a month working in the Indian leather industry just to be able to get into the shoes (literally) of one of his key protagonists, a shoemaker. For me, this is a form of 'method writing' in the way actors such as Daniel Day Lewis employ method acting.

Historical crime writing rarely makes such onerous demands on its creators – but the research effort demanded by a historical mystery should not be underestimated.

The Importance of Themes

Why are humans so bad at learning lessons from history? Why do we seem doomed to repeat the same mistakes?

My own theory is that this happens because, at a global level, we are incredibly poor at teaching history, or at least the history that truly matters. And we are equally bad at distilling lessons from history and then instilling that learning in future generations.

My Malabar House novels seeks to teach readers about the British time in India and the lessons that might be learned about colonialism. They also reflect the place of women in an intensely patriarchal society, as India in the 1950s was and, as some argue, still is. These are debates we are still engaged in today.

Historical fiction allows the exploration of such themes better than any other genre, in my opinion, because it manages to link what we can see happening around us in the present with the past.

I know for a fact that readers appreciate this. They may not agree with our take on a particular subject, but the fact that we have tabled for discussion matters of import – whilst entertaining them with a healthy dose of murderous mystery fiction – often elevates our offerings above other fare.

* * *

Like every mystery novel, an essay such as this demands a satisfying conclusion, wrapping up the various strands explored in the work. This piece has examined the what and the why of historical mystery fiction's popularity. For me, there is something else that binds the historical novelist to the crime fiction novelist – the search for truth.

Crime fiction's protagonists seek justice – but in so doing they must uncover the truth behind what, initially, appears to be a complicated and intractably puzzling set of circumstances. This search for truth is little different from the manner in which historians – and historical fiction writers – piece together the past, a process of unearthing clues, making extrapolations, and using deductive reasoning to fill in the gaps.

In the 1930s, a Bengali writer named Sharadindu Bandyopadhyay introduced us to India's answer to Sherlock Holmes: Byomkesh Bakshi, an observant, hyper-intelligent sleuth solving crimes in Calcutta, a man whose analytical skills and expertise in forensic science were routinely utilised by the local police force, much like the character that inspired his creation. Bakshi went on to feature in more than thirty stories over four decades with several big and small screen incarnations.

Bakshi referred to himself as *satyanweshi* – meaning 'truth seeker'.

Today's historical crime novelists are truth seekers, too; but the truth they seek is broader than the answer to a mystery. It encompasses a wider search for the truth of a particular period, a setting within that period, and the characters that people that period.

Breaking the Translation Barrier

Quentin Bates

The row of hardbacks with the weird names was on the second shelf from the top. It was years before I had any real idea of how to pronounce Sjöwall & Wahlöö, but the stories themselves became an instant addiction.

This was way back in the 1970s, when this curious young teenager had outgrown Biggles, had already made a dent in Simenon, and was searching Mum's bookshelves for something interesting. The seedy world of Martin Beck and his Stockholm police colleagues was quickly devoured, all ten of the series.

There was nothing of the gentility of British crime fiction about the recurring characters, and neither was there the machismo of American cops, although these were definitely closer to Ed McBain than Agatha Christie – and the ambience was closer to Maigret and his henchmen. It was easy to become engrossed in the world of Martin Beck and the characters around him: reliable Lennart Kollberg, the quick-tempered and flashy Gunvald Larsson, unimaginative Rönn, and Melander, somehow always in the toilet when he's needed. There's a revolving cast of additional characters – Månsson from down south in Malmö appears only a couple of times, Stenström who was killed halfway through the series, and his bereft girlfriend Åsa Torell who later joins the force.

Then there are the idiots, the inept uniformed officers Kvant and Kristiansson, who muddle through, ruining crime scenes by barging through them and generally being far from competent. After Kvant's death midway through the series, Kristiansson is partnered with the equally incompetent but lamentably enthusiastic Kvastmo.

Part of the charm and possibly the realism of the books is that they don't shy away from incompetence. Wrong turns, false trails and investigations being bungled are themes that run through the stories, right up to Zachrisson's monumental blunder, managing to get the Prime Minister assassinated on his watch.

The interplay between them is deft, showing an extent of the personal lives of these characters that wasn't usual in crime fiction at the time, not least as Martin Beck's marriage falls apart, his relationship with his children evolves in different directions, and he finds happiness in a new relationship – as well as being seriously injured in the course of his work and being promoted beyond his own comfort zone.

Refreshingly, the characters created by Sjöwall & Wahlöö frequently don't like each other, or even get on. At one point, Kollberg describes Larsson as 'the stupidest detective in the history of criminal investigation', and makes his point even more forcefully later on in the series – before leaving the force as his convictions become too strong for his conscience.

The husband-and-wife pair of journalists Maj Sjöwall and Per Wahlöö between them wrote ten stories about Martin Beck and his circle of colleagues and friends between *Roseanna* in 1965 and *The Terrorists* in 1975, the year of Per Wahlöö's death. The story is that they didn't set out to write bestsellers, but in fact had Marxist sympathies and wanted to present an incisive warts-and-all critique of Swedish society and its problems, using a police detective framework as their vehicle. The books became bestsellers, and not only in Sweden, earning them far more in royalties than they had ever imagined or were comfortable with.

There have been translations into dozens of languages, radio dramas, and a stack of screen adaptations over the years.

Probably without meaning to, Sjöwall and Wahlöö were the forerunners who set a template for the way Nordic crime fiction evolved, with a big-picture viewpoint over a series of novels, giving their flawed and not always likeable characters all the space they needed to mature and change, all entwined with an apparently impenetrable crime and with a more-or-less satisfying dénouement.

What's also remarkable about these ten novels is how fresh they remain, fifty-odd years on from their creation. Apart from the lack of computers and mobile phones, the fact that policemen catch buses and smoking is practically compulsory, these books are as lively and relevant as much that's appearing today – and Sjöwall & Wahlöö showed that less can be more.

There's a colossal affection for Sjöwall & Wahlöö that extends far beyond their native Sweden. There's barely a crime writer in the Nordic region who won't admit to owing a debt of gratitude to this pair. Norwegian author Jørn Lier Horst became a real detective with a long police career after having immersed himself in Martin Beck as a boy. Swedish writer Åsa Larsson went so far as to hide Martin Beck's name within that of her own protagonist, RecBECKa MARTINsson.

So what happened next? Well, for us anglophone readers, that was it. There was no more Nordic crime fiction to be had in English.

This left me with a lifelong habit of scanning library and bookshop shelves for odd names, and that turned up quite a few gems from far-flung places – Josef Škvorecký's compact tales of Czech policeman Lieutenant Boruvka, Jean-Claude Izzo's magnificent, chaotic Marseilles trilogy. But as far as Scandinavian detectives were concerned, that's all there was.

There was crime fiction in the Nordic region before Sjöwall & Wahlöö – but none of this made it into translation, and it was a good while before anything else emerged to follow these forerunners. It's notable that this is a situation that applies particularly to us English-language readers. For whatever reason, British and American publishers have long had (and often still have) a suspicious reluctance to publish translated fiction. It's still the case that around a quarter of the titles on the shelves of a bookshop in France or Germany will be translated from English or elsewhere, but in a British or American bookshop no more than five per cent originate from another language.

So readers in French, German, Dutch, Czech and other languages had access to fiction from other parts of the world, including the Nordic countries, for years before Peter Høeg's Miss Smilla made her appearance in English and began to turn things around.

We can't say much about Nordic crime fiction in English without mentioning Christopher MacLehose, the veteran publisher with a gimlet eye for talent in translation who brought us *Miss Smilla's Feeling for Snow* in the early 1990s, which now feels like a lifetime ago. This was followed by Henning Mankell's tales of troubled Ystad detective Kurt Wallender, the first of which appeared in English in 1997. He also sniffed out the *Girl with the Dragon Tattoo* series of novels written by the colourful and complex Stieg Larsson, who had intended a longer series for his protagonist Lisbeth Salander, but just three had been completed by the time he died in 2004. The original Millennium Trilogy has since been followed by more of the same brand, with several other writers drafted in to fill the big shoes Larsson unexpectedly left behind.

With Lisbeth Salander on the loose and romping up the bestseller lists, *The Killing* and *The Bridge* on our TV screens, and publishers scrabbling for more Scandinavian talent as we got into the 2010s, Nordic noir had arrived in Britain and the US, and it's still very much with us, now an established genre rather than a quirky, soon-to-disappear niche.

From its very Swedish roots, Nordic noir has expanded in all sorts of directions. Publishers in Britain hunted around for unpublished Swedish writers, and cast the net wider to Norway and Denmark, as well as to Finland – and to Iceland. That's where I come into the saga of Nordic noir.

Back in the 1990s, a publisher who had clearly searched hard for someone who could speak Icelandic (which in itself is a long story) asked for a critique and a synopsis of *Sons of the Dust*, a debut novel by an Icelandic film critic called Arnaldur Indriðason. A year or two later, they came back for another reader report for a different novel. Of course, I obliged and reported back that the first book had some interesting characters, but the plot was on the far-fetched side. The second one, a pacier, US-style series of cliffhangers, got much the same report. Of the two, *Sons of the Dust* remains untranslated, but *Operation Napoleon* made it into print years later, and has subsequently become a movie.

Iceland's own brand of crime fiction goes back a long way, to *An Icelandic Sherlock Holmes* stories written by Jóhann Magnús Bjarnason in the early years of the twentieth century, and followed by novels such as *The House by the North River* by Einar Skálaglamm (Guðbrandur Jónsson) in 1926, *All's Well in Reykjavík* by Ólafur við Faxafen (Ólafur Friðriksson) in 1939, and a series of stories by Valentínus (Steindór Sigurðsson) in the 1930s and Valur Vestan (Steingrímur Sigfússon) in the 1940s. These novels were written under pseudonyms. Maybe this was because crime fiction was then – as it was until fairly recently – seen as an inferior class of literature they preferred not to admit to writing.

During the 1980s and '90s, according to the annals of the Icelandic Crime Syndicate, new writers produced crime fiction, this time writing under their own names, Viktor Arnar Ingólfsson, Gunnar Gunnarsson, Birgitta H Halldórsdóttir and a handful of others. Towards the end of the '90s, there are some new names – including Arnaldur Indriðason, whose debut novel featuring detective Erlendur Sveinsson didn't produce many ripples. It was *Mýrin*, published in English as *Jar City*, that made readers and critics sit up and take notice, and even more so when the eerily dark, atmospheric film appeared, made by an Icelandic production company and partly using as its backdrop a part of Iceland that right now has a newly restless volcano looming over it.

There's no doubt that Arnaldur was the one who made the breakthrough into translation – into English, German, French and more. There's also no doubt that his English translator, the late Bernard Scudder, bears much of the responsibility for rendering Arnaldur's prose into a smooth, highly readable English that loses none of the brooding atmosphere of the original. A poet himself and a long-time resident in Iceland, Bernard Scudder was the Central Bank's in-house translator in addition to working on fiction, and also brought Yrsa Sigurðardóttir's uniquely dark novels into English – and was still hard at work until his untimely death in 2007.

Arnaldur and Yrsa have been the big hitters of the Icelandic crime fiction scene. It has become a staple event of the publishing year for their novels to appear on the first of November. The latest Arnaldur, or this year's Yrsa, becomes a topic of conversation in canteens and around office water coolers for a few weeks as people discuss the relative merits of both in the weeks leading up to Christmas, when a book is the default safe option gift, in an amicable competition engineered by their publishers to jostle for the top slot on the bestseller lists.

They were also, for quite some years, practically the only crime fiction from Iceland that made it into English, even though they and plenty of others had been translated into German, French, and other languages. We anglophone readers were yet again left trailing behind the rest of Europe.

There has been something of a change in recent years, as veteran crime writer Viktor Arnar Ingólfsson made an appearance in English, and then along came Ragnar Jónasson (now a mega-seller in a dozen languages as well as English), Lilja Sigurðardóttir, Óskar Guðmundsson, Sólveig Pálsdóttir, Eva Björg Ægisdóttir, the mysteriously anonymous Stella Blómkvist and more, as if the floodgates had finally opened and it had been accepted that writers from this part of the world were worth translating into English – although there are some who inexplicably have yet to make it into translation, notably veterans Ævar Örn Jósepsson, Árni Thórarinsson, Stefán Máni and Guðrún Guðlaugsdóttir.

On top of all this is a wave of new writing in this genre in Iceland. Until relatively recently, there had genuinely only been a modest group of Icelandic authors who regularly turned out crime novels. It wasn't that long ago that the bestseller lists in Iceland, especially around the Christmas book season, were dominated by biographies of worthy figures, literary novels – and crime fiction, but translated from English or some other language.

The axiom of nobody being a prophet in their own land holds pretty true here. It wasn't until Arnaldur, Yrsa and a few others had been acclaimed as real talents by readers and critics outside Iceland, and later when series such as *Trapped* hit the TV screens, that the feeling really changed and writers of crime fiction began to be taken seriously. Today there's a surfeit of home-grown crime fiction, and this regularly hits the top spots on the bestseller lists. The styles range from straightforward procedurals to cosy crime to gory in the extreme. Every taste is catered for.

It's taken a while for crime fiction to become accepted (mostly) as mainstream, the kind of stuff that civilised people can admit to reading. One of the traits of Icelandic society is that things aren't done by halves, and these days – to paraphrase Wodehouse – you can hardly chuck a brick in Reykjavík without hitting a crime writer.

* * *

I'm one of a small group of Nordic pretenders. There's a long tradition of writers in English setting their work in far-flung locations. Most have the sense to do this in places where the sun shines, the sea is blue, and the cuisine is exquisite. Others of us, for a variety of reasons, have headed northwards, where the sea can turn from cobalt blue to a furious windswept grey in a matter of minutes and the sun shines brightly at midnight in May when you'd really like to get to sleep. Let's not go into the cuisine.

Christoffer Pettersen sets his books in Greenland, where he lived and worked as a teacher before settling in Denmark. Jan Costin Wagner is from Germany, but sets his stories in Finland. Torquil Macleod's series of novels centred around detective Anita Sundström are set in the colourful Swedish city of Malmö. Michael Ridpath found Iceland as a location for his thrillers – and then there's me. After living in Iceland for many years, when the urge to write became irresistible, then it had to be set on the island that had been home for so long, and is again.

Since side-stepping into translation as well, I've become almost more at home in the stories other people create than in my own, and it's still an odd feeling.

Having also done quite a bit of technical and news material translation, this step sideways into fiction was also a jump into new territory. Technical stuff is all about precision – knowing the difference in both languages between a crankshaft and a camshaft – and rendering the English text into something as close as possible to the original, leaving nothing open to doubt or misinterpretation. But fiction has turned out to be different. That precision is still very much needed – but it's a case of delivering what the author would have written if he or she had written it in English. There's more flexibility and it's more about what the author meant to say than precisely how it's said. Give the same text to two translators, and they'll probably each come up with something different as they interpret in their own ways. That's the crux of it: rendering fiction into another language is more interpretation than strictly translation.

The language itself isn't enough – which is why machine translation will (hopefully) not replace a human translator. As well as an affinity for both subject and target languages, an understanding of the cultural nuances has to be there — which is the trashy newspaper, what undertone a mention of this or that district conveys, the place a particular public figure occupies in the national psyche – and a translator should be able to slip in discreet explanations, a word or a phrase, without interrupting the flow.

This isn't a 2+2=4 state of affairs. The idiosyncrasies of language are such that there are words and concepts that don't translate easily. What can be an expression in one language might be a single word in another, and there are neat, compact words in Icelandic that need several in English to do them justice. *Frekja* is one such, meaning an awkward, entitled bloody-mindedness, and how it's translated also depends on the context it's used in, whether it's belligerent or simply pushy. It's such a useful word that there should be a direct English equivalent.

The fun really starts when it comes to jokes and plays on words. That's when there's the dilemma of translating faithfully, providing a precise version of the author's words, or of coming up with an alternative which may be something very different but delivers the right mood or feel, and which has the advantage of being funny – which was the author's intention to begin with. It's a question of being faithful to the author's words, or to the author's meaning.

Translators into English from any Nordic language are also in something of a special position. This wasn't so much the case when I came to Iceland in the 1970s, but today you would struggle to find anyone under fifty who doesn't have at least a functional command of English. In fact, English has become so widespread there's a real possibility that the Icelandic language as we know it right now could well join the ranks of dead languages within a generation or two. Icelandic authors tend to speak a US-slanted English with a ready fluency, and a confidence that means that when some idiom or quirk in the text catches their eye, the assumption is invariably not that this could be an unfamiliar expression or a form of words they simply haven't previously encountered, but that the translator has got it wrong.

Most authors are anxious to cast an eye over what the translator has done. I understand this perfectly, having been in this position as a couple of my books have been translated, and I naturally wanted to see how my babies were transformed. There should be a to-and-fro between author and translator. Most are keen to answer questions and bat ideas back and forth, or even suggest changes or additions. It's rare, but some don't engage, or even respond at all. Some send a manuscript back studded with comments and criss-crossed with well-meaning tracked changes that can be valid contributions, or can introduce a whole new slew of errors and misunderstandings. Others respond with a single line: 'That's fine. Thank you!'

The third side of the triangle is the editor, and in general editors can be more of a headache than authors, as they're the outsiders without access to the original words. At any rate, I've never yet worked with an editor who can read the original text.

So this is where errors and misunderstandings are more likely to slip in and the translator, to an extent, has to defend what they've done and sometimes kick back when the editor reworks something in a way that's out of keeping with the original, or tries to make a story into something it isn't.

Worst of all is when a publisher has bought a book unread that turns out to be less than brilliant, and the expectation is that the translator will sprinkle some fairy dust over it and turn it into a masterpiece. That's when it's time to go back to the author, and not ask the translator to work miracles. An inspired translation can make a good book into something that sings, but no amount of translation skill turns a mongrel into a pedigree prize winner.

* * *

Are the robots taking over? The Artificial Intelligence cat is long out of the bag. In reality, it has been for a long time. Machine learning has implications for so much of our daily lives, and undoubtedly has the potential to do great things and make our lives easier and more comfortable, although there's also the spectre of what this technology could do to screw things up for us.

Computers fed with enough raw data can generate stories of their own and convincingly mimic styles. Just because they can't yet deliver a plot that hangs together doesn't mean that they won't eventually be able to do so. I'm aware that several of my own books and more than a few translations have already been mined by the tech behemoths for just this, and it's uncomfortable to know that this has been done without a word – with permission neither asked nor given.

Google and other translation engines have been around for a good few years already, and these unquestionably have their uses. The question is whether translators will become redundant in future.

Quite some years ago, I dropped a slab of text into an online translator to see what would happen, and was reassured by the abysmal gobbledygook that came out. A few days ago, I tried the same experiment, and was startled to see just how much this particular translation machine has improved. That's not to say that the outcome was sparkling text, but it was so much better than it had been just a few years ago.

This is already coming to the world of fiction. Translators in some fields are already being asked to check and polish text that has been machine translated. I'm dreading the first such request to come my way, and from what I've seen so far, my gut feeling is that the checking and editing process is going to be at least as time-consuming as a translation from scratch – and far less fun. I'm dreading the first such request to turn a piece of fiction into something good enough to be published from text a computer has spat out in a matter of seconds, and I know what I'll say.

Translation is a fairly substantial cost, especially for a niche novel that doesn't sell in huge numbers, and publishers will see this as a way to cut costs, and also to get things done faster – which is ironic for an industry in which everything already moves at the pace of a snail that's in no particular hurry. I was going to say: when this comes, it's going to be about money. But it's already here, and it remains to be seen how well machine translation works with the nuances of fiction.

I don't doubt that the instructions for a tumble dryer could be translated competently enough by a machine. A translation computer won't miss a beat in telling the difference between a crankshaft and a camshaft – but it's less likely to sense the blurry line between impertinence and cheek.

Those who will miss out will be the readers, who are going to lose those subtleties and quirks that make literature what it is.

Cop Stuff: Fact or Fantasy

Paul Finch

Two of the most common questions faced by the crime fiction writing community are: How accurate are your police procedurals? And/or: Do you go out of your way to make them as true to life as possible? My short answer to the latter question would be that 'some of us do, and some of us don't'. But a short answer is inadequate. Because this is a more complex issue than the average person might think, and there are many shades of grey within it. And yet it's equally the case that it's not necessarily as crucial to the creation of an effective crime novel as one might believe.

To start with, let's roll back the years a little…

One of the world's most instantly recognisable fictional police officers is Inspector Harry Callahan, aka 'Dirty Harry', of the San Francisco Police Department. The central protagonist in five movies, twelve spin-off novels, and at least two video games, Callahan is infamous the world over as an embittered loner of a homicide detective, who adopts such a merciless approach to his duty that during the course of it, he shoots and kills a total of forty-three criminals.

Now, you don't have to be a sceptic to feel fairly sure that, even back in the rough and ready 1970s, it would be inconceivable for any police officer serving anywhere in the civilised world to have such a body count to his name. Yet, even now, fifty years after the first one was released, the *Dirty Harry* films are screened regularly and remain hugely popular. Movie and crime-thriller fans the world over regard Inspector Harry Callahan as the benchmark tough cop, the law enforcement individual who, more than any other, takes the battle to the underworld.

I'm not suggesting, of course, that as an archetype Harry Callahan was real, or even that he *should* have been real. But so well written and directed were the *Dirty Harry* movies (by, among others, Don Siegal, Harry Julian Fink, John Milius, Michael Cimino, etc.), and so iconically performed by Clint Eastwood, the overall package so enthralling, that the nonsensical nature of the central concept has never counted for much. If a new series of *Dirty Harry* films or novels was to emerge today, the crowds would lap them up the same way they did half a century ago.

So, I guess the big question this poses is: does it actually matter if a central police character in a work of fiction is even remotely realistic?

Before we attempt to answer that, perhaps we should also ask ourselves how realistic many of the other fictionalised portrayals of the police are, including those who are significantly less radical than Harry Callahan, even those who wear their 'realism' as a badge of honour.

I was a cop before I became a writer, so I'm reasonably well positioned to make a judgement on this. Even more so, perhaps, because my first professional writing job was penning scripts for *The Bill*, the long-running British drama from Thames Television, concerning Sun Hill, a fictional police subdivision in the East End of London.

The Bill, which focused on the characters of one particular relief and their counterparts in CID, prided itself on being as close to real life as possible. Okay, it was a work of drama, not True Crime; no one suggested otherwise. But it was very important to the show's producers that the police procedures and protocols were bang on, and that British policing as it existed in the 1980s and '90s was replicated as closely as possible. New writers who didn't have police experience were encouraged to go on police drive-alongs, so they could experience at first hand the kind of jobs that uniform and detective officers encounter on a day-to-day basis, while official police advisors were attached permanently to the show. In nearly all cases these were experienced ex-cops themselves, who would provide detailed guidance and information throughout the whole production process.

In contrast to another popular British cop show of a decade earlier, *The Sweeney*, which was really a pacy action series rather than a police procedural, *The Bill* prided itself on being as close as damn it to the real thing.

But how real was it actually? And how real could it ever be?

Just off the top of my head, there are several reasons why film and TV police dramas will always struggle to be absolutely accurate.

COP STUFF: FACT OR FANTASY

First of all, they are dramas. They are in the business of telling rattling good stories, not to mention following the fortunes of certain selected characters, putting them at the heart of the action no matter what twists and turns the narrative takes. In both these cases, some realities will need to be sidelined, and we're not just talking *The Bill* now. We're talking crime and police fiction across a wide range of media.

Consider this. Most divisional uniforms are too busy with routine assignments, which they are landed with throughout their shift, to focus on one particular case. They certainly would not continue to investigate serious crime, as that would be handed over to supervision, then to CID, and finally, maybe, to a specialist unit. Their involvement from that point on would be peripheral. Likewise, many authors' and screenwriters' central police hero is the ubiquitous DI, or detective inspector, who always gets his or her man however heinous the crime. But heading up a murder enquiry, for example, is rarely a detective inspector's responsibility. Yes, the DI has a senior investigative role, but if anything, it's a kind of middle management position. There would most certainly be DIs involved in a murder enquiry, but it would be extremely rare for them to be in charge of it. So, bearing these inconvenient realities in mind, how do you make your DI, never mind your PC, the centre-point of a story involving the hunt for an extremely villainous villain? Well, the most frequently leapt-for answer should be obvious: for as long as it matters, you ditch the house rule wherein everything must be super-realistic, and proceed with the story the way you want to tell it.

And this happens in the film, TV and book-writing world time and again. And as with the most extreme version of it, *Dirty Harry*, very few consumers seem to care.

Now, if the mere thought of that gives you the shivers, and you really, urgently want to emphasise fact not fantasy, bear in mind that it would make you something of a rarity. There are many aspects of policework that simply don't lend themselves to good fiction.

Much of a police officer's day, and this applies to uniformed coppers as well as detectives, involves waiting around. You might be on surveillance, which is rarely as romantic as it is often portrayed, and in fact can be tedious and often brings no result. Alternatively, you could be marooned in the custody suite, waiting for a solicitor or social worker to turn up, or you could be at the hospital waiting to interview a witness, or the victim of the crime itself, or, most boring of all, you could be handcuffed to the suspect because they are in need of medical attention too.

On top of all this, of course, there is the infamous mountain of paperwork. Strictly speaking, it's not paperwork these days. It's all done electronically. But the world of law enforcement is a bureaucrat's dream. There are forms to fill in for everything, reports to be made and filed, statements to be signed and so on. Then there is the matter of exam-taking. It's rare that younger police officers aren't studying towards some exam or other, and so will fit moments of revision in whenever they can. (Granted, this doesn't take precedence over actually doing the job, but if you are on an obbo, for example, and nothing's happening, or if it's a quiet day and you're simply parked up, waiting on the next call, it's not uncommon to try and get some study time in.)

As you can imagine, none of this, relayed in detail, would make for compelling crime-fighting fiction. So, most authors skimp on it.

But there are other areas too where liberties are taken.

Consider crime scene procedure. Every man and his dog thinks he knows how crime scenes are handled, because they've seen it done so often in films and on television, but film and TV dramas are among the worst offenders when it comes to representing crime scene protocols. For one thing, head-to-foot protective clothing must invariably be worn at a live crime scene, and you don't always see that. For another, even the investigating detectives will need to stay off the scene until the SCIs and the other techs have performed their own vital duties. You don't often see that either. By the way, I don't mention these errors because I condone them. I'm just pointing out that short-cutting reality like this is not at all uncommon in the world of crime fiction. That said, there are certain aspects of police life and policework that writers, in my view, really should try to get right.

The first of these is very important, and that is command structure. The very last thing a British author should do is ape the order of rank that we see in American movies, talking about lieutenants, captains and so on. That is only one of many big differences between the police world in the UK and the police world in the US.

With very few variations, the British police ranking structure is as follows, from the bottom up: constable, sergeant, inspector, chief inspector, superintendent, chief superintendent. Above chief superintendent, you move into the realms where there are some differences between forces and between certain specialised departments. For example, one squad might be under the control of a 'commander', while another might defer to a 'director'. In addition, of course, you have the most senior ranks. Again in ascending order, these tend to be the assistant chief constable, the deputy chief constable, and the chief constable (unless you're in the City of London Police, wherein the overarching power is the commander, or the Metropolitan Police, i.e. Greater London, where it's the commissioner).

Within CID it is much the same. You start with detective constable, then move up through detective sergeant, detective inspector, detective chief inspector, detective superintendent and detective chief superintendent. Above that, as before, you may have a commander or director, depending on which department or unit you are concerned with. Also – and this is very important – in England and Wales, it's not the case that 'detective' is a rank all of its own (again, as we often see in American movies). In Britain, a detective constable has no more authority than a uniformed constable, nor a detective sergeant than a uniformed sergeant and so on. However, police detectives occupy a very specialised role within the job, which only experienced officers are usually admitted to. So, it wouldn't be unusual for a degree of deference to be shown towards them by the other rank and file. In addition, even a detective constable might, if he or she is recognised for having certain expertise, be allocated tactical command for specific operations.

Another area in which I'd consider it important not to make mistakes, is that of legality... and not just in terms of what constitutes a crime, but also what constitutes a legal police response to it. For example, whether or not a power of arrest exists, whether a search is permissible, whether a warrant is required, and so forth. While minor police procedures and protocols (internal discipline, radio procedure and such) change all the time, and vary from one force area to the next, in which case it's not always possible for a writer to stay completely in line with everything, the actual law changes less speedily, and when it does change it's easier to keep track of it.

When I first commenced my writing career, every time I stumbled upon something I was uncertain about, it necessitated a trip to the local reference library and hours spent leafing through dusty legal tomes. But these days, we have the internet, which is particularly good for law. It's all online in black and white. So, while the routines of local police stations may change often and out of sight of the general public, there is no excuse for authors to make howlers when it comes to larger legal matters. For example, you are rarely going to need to quote the act and subsection under which your police hero is arresting a suspect, but it's certainly worth familiarising yourself with which offences do and don't exist. No one in England and Wales these days gets arrested for larceny (unless you're in the Channel Islands), or sexual battery, or grand theft auto (which are all purely American terms). Making errors like these will stand out.

The same could probably be said for forensics and technology.

The biggest mistake made with the former is that authors often overestimate it. Some US cop shows verge on being science fiction, and I strongly recommend in-depth research rather than repeating some technique you saw on the telly, which looked almost too fantastical to be true (because at the very least, you'll have seen an oversimplified version of it). But by the same token, the acquisition of DNA evidence is absolutely vital in today's war on crime, and methods have improved exponentially in recent years. If your criminals don't take account of that, they aren't going to stay at liberty for very long; or if they do, your book is not going to be taken seriously.

Even some of crime fiction's true masters have taken liberties to absurd levels.

In Alfred Hitchcock's 1972 movie *Frenzy*, there is a scene in which Bob Rusk, the serial necktie strangler who has been terrorising London's West End, climbs into the back of a potato truck to retrieve a tie pin from his most recent victim. He is all over the body in his efforts to extricate the vital clue from her stiffened grasp, later climbing from the vehicle, dishevelled and covered in potato dust, to call a taxi from a nearby truck stop (where there are witnesses present), the car then taking him back to his home neighbourhood in London.

Don't get me wrong. It's a very tense moment in a terrific thriller, and makes for edge-of-the-seat viewing, but even in an era when DNA was unknown, any murderer behaving so recklessly would have been in custody within a day or so, maybe less. Fibres and fingerprints would have been left everywhere, alongside possible blood traces. And that's before we even consider that the offender makes minimal effort to conceal himself from other patrons at the truck stop. In contrast, real murderers who are active today, specifically those who do it for a living, i.e. hitmen, often carry out their crimes gloved, with their features concealed, perhaps even with their ears and nostrils plugged to prevent any fragments of their person being left behind for some inquisitive crime scene investigator to find.

That's the level of crime scene technology we're now dealing with. If you commit a murder, a droplet of sweat could send you to prison for life, never mind a splash of your blood or semen. You may wonder how sex killers ever get away with it. Well, the truth is that most of them don't. In the twenty-first century, the rate of serial murder is down significantly on the 1990s and especially the 1980s, which, thus far, was the peak decade for that kind of fiendish activity. Most likely, this is not because there is any shortage of killers, but because detection rates have vastly improved for all the reasons we have discussed. If you're going to write about something that would elicit a massive police response with an enormous budget behind it, such as an enquiry into a possible series of murders, you must take all this into account.

Other forms of tech have also now come into play, and this effects more routine criminal offences, like drug dealing, robbery and car theft.

Many of Britain's roadside cameras are now equipped with number plate recognition software, all subsequent data fed into a central computer, which will immediately flag up anomalies. You can't just drive around in a car that's been reported stolen anymore. Likewise, a car that's been fitted with false number plates, but which isn't the same make and model, may be noted before it's even been used in a crime. The same goes for facial recognition technology. In the UK, we are a heavily surveilled society. Walk along any high street and you are likely to be captured on camera repeatedly. So, if you want to rob a bank and hope to get away with it, you can't just put a mask on round the corner, then go running in with gun in hand. Under the current system, investigators will be able to track your movements both before and after the crime, maybe even to your own front door.

Again, all these things need to be considered when you are writing your crime novel. Ignore them if you wish. Call to mind that old adage, 'don't let the facts get in the way of a good story'. But whereas that is probably okay if you're just ignoring one of those dratted but minor police protocols that we've already talked about, larger exclusions like these could leave you open to criticism and maybe even mockery.

But still, we are in the business of telling fantastical tales, are we not?

We're not writing police textbooks. In fact, we are constantly seeking to fill our work with jeopardy, excitement and intrigue. We definitely do *not* want to get bogged down in legal, procedural or technical minutiae. The trick, therefore, is to work your way around these things. Okay, we've already seen that there are certain things you can simply get away with. The public are too used to seeing DIs running murder enquiries to object. Even as a senior detective, it's highly unlikely you'd be attached to an investigation into the murder of someone close

COP STUFF: FACT OR FANTASY

to you, such as a colleague or family member, but it happens often on the screen, so it's probably not a mortal sin if it also happens in your novel.

But my personal view is that the book will only benefit if you can find valid reasons why such protocols are set aside.

To offer an example, at first my DS Mark 'Heck' Heckenburg series concept presented me with a conundrum. I did not want a police hero who was confined to a particular subdivision in a particular town, with no possibility of his venturing beyond those boundaries. I thus invented the National Crime Group – and before anyone asks, this was prior to the creation of the real-life National Crime Agency, so I always say that they pinched the idea from me.

In the Heck novels, the National Crime Group is a special investigations department with a remit to cover all the police areas of England and Wales. Primarily, of course, NCG officers would be liaising with local forces rather than investigating off their own bat, but this still gave me the opportunity to send Heck, my main protagonist, all over the country, to different locations in each book. So, for example, in the first one, *Stalkers*, he visits the Home Counties, Lancashire and Kent. In the second book, *Sacrifice*, it's Manchester and the Cotswolds; in the third book, *The Killing Club*, he finishes up in the north-east of England, Holy Island, in fact; and in the most recent one, *Kiss of Death*, the East End of London, Humberside and Cornwall.

It was also the case that I wanted Heck to be a lead investigator, but not a senior officer. My solution therefore was to make him a detective sergeant, which gave him some authority but no political pull, but also to load him with such expertise that he would add great value to any local force's investigation into a complex crime. To cement this, I divided the National Crime Group into three subsections: the Kidnap Squad, the Organised Crime Division and the Serial Crimes Unit. I made Heck part of the latter, which meant he could investigate serial murders all around England and Wales, and pursue roving killers across police force boundaries, in each volume in company with a different set of supporting characters.

Now, 'Whoa!' you might be saying. 'Hold your horses! What do you mean you *invented* the National Crime Group? How is that permissible?'

Well, it's permissible because I'm the author. And yes, I *invented* it. These are crime novels, works of fiction. You're entitled to invent stuff and can expect your readership to suspend belief sufficiently to take it seriously, so long as it's the sort of thing that *could* exist within the conventional police universe. So, to continue with my own example, no one is going to object too much to Heck being part of a specialist nationwide serial murder team (not when, in the States, the FBI possesses units like VICAP, the Violent Criminal Apprehension Programme), whereas they probably would object if Heck went out to assist local forces by flying car rather than catching the train like everyone else.

Of course, I'm not the only thriller writer to do this. There are other, more glaring examples.

One particularly good one is FX TV's *The Shield* (2002–08), regarded by many as one of the best cop shows of all time, though it was not without controversy. It focused on the LAPD's anti-gang unit, the Strike Team, who would break every rule to bring their own brand of justice to the tough Farmington district. In reality, there is no such entity as the Strike Team, and no such place as Farmington, but Shawn Ryan, who created the show, based it on the real-life Rampart Division of an earlier era, some of whose members used ultra strongarm tactics to control the streets in Downtown LA, and in so doing, fell foul of many laws themselves. *Shield* audiences were left agog at the sight of central police characters committing every offence under the sun, including murder, robbery and even torture, and continually getting away with it, but they were more able to accept it because something similar – though not exactly the same – had happened for real.

However, less realistic by far were Ian Fleming's James Bond novels, even though they were a soaraway success, as of course were the films in later decades. From the outset, we can probably all guess that in the post-World War Two era, there has never been any such thing as a 00 'license to kill' designation (at least, none that the British Government would ever admit to). But the factor of the Cold War, and probably a significant degree of wishful thinking, enabled readers and film audiences to suppress all critical thought and simply enjoy the Bond stories for what they were. Similarly, Sherlock Holmes, a consulting detective, was basically a private eye, but a PI whom Scotland Yard sometimes (even regularly) deferred to. Most crime fiction fans will know without needing to be told that this would never have happened in reality, but such was the enjoyment to be had from Conan Doyle's compelling narratives that any notion of implausibility is set aside. It's the same with the 'cosy crime' phenomenon, both present day and Golden Age, in which many murder cases are resolved by deductions so clever they verge on the genius, but don't come with anything like enough evidence for a successful prosecution to have been mounted.

Ultimately, though, all I can offer here are a few thoughts and suggestions.

You are the person writing the book, so *you* are the one in charge of what appears there, and if it's too outlandish, *you* will be the one who'll need to explain it to your editors.

But there is one area in which they'll never be able to call you out, even if they are particularly zealous. And this is in terms of the characters you employ. Because the best books are always about people, and cop thrillers are no exception. In fact, on this front, cop thrillers give you an extraordinary opportunity.

One thing about the police world that is *not* fantasy, and never has been – and this is where you as a writer can absolutely make hay! – is that police officers are, for the most part, ordinary men and women thrust regularly into extraordinary circumstances. Even back in my day, when there were many more ex-military in the police than now (most of them Northern Ireland and Falklands War veterans, and thus rugged customers by any standards), the majority of officers had previously been plumbers, teachers, shop assistants, sales personnel, postal workers, electricians, etc. Name any commonplace job you want, and that was the world they'd inhabited before they

COP STUFF: FACT OR FANTASY

donned the uniform. Myself, I'd only ever been a student; being a copper was my first full-time job.

It's even more the case now, and what this means is that inside the police service there is a plethora of everyday people, drawn from all ages, races and creeds, but all of whom are dedicated to confronting the forces of lawlessness, with all the darkness, stress and fear that implies. So, just look at the scope for drama and tension that this offers you as the writer.

And feel free to take it to the extreme.

In my DC Lucy Clayburn novel, *Shadows*, my blue-collar Manchester-based heroine found herself engaged in a motorbike pursuit along a busy railway line. In my Heck novel, *Dead Man Walking*, the hunt for a spree killer up in the Lake District is bedevilled by an impenetrable winter fog. And none of these situations can be dismissed as fantasy, because they are all based on real events.

It's an old phrase – almost a cliché, in fact – but when you're in the cops, the truth can be much stranger than fiction.

What we're in the business of here is building intricate, intriguing stories about men and women, just like us rather than superheroes, who face a weekly diet of murder, mystery and mayhem, who are often in peril themselves, who deal daily with people suffering terrible trauma, and of course who must able to laugh and joke about it when the pressure is off, sometimes over a drink or ten, and yet who then must go home to spouses, partners, children and try to live as normal a private life as possible.

Personally, I can't think of anything else in the civilian experience that offers such a range of possibilities for a fiction writer looking to absolutely hook his or her audience. It's not just a physical ordeal your heroes are going to endure, it's psychological, emotional, even spiritual. You can attack them (and your readers!) on every level. And again, I reiterate, no one can say that this part of the crime-writing job is fantasy rather than fact, because it absolutely isn't.

So, if there's anything to take from all this, it's don't be put off by the onerous-seeming possibility that your cop novel won't be realistic enough. I'm now decades out of the job, and things have changed astoundingly. The police life I knew was closer to *Life on Mars* than the modern service. So, I must do my research like everyone else. And honestly, it's not that hard. Everything you need to know is out there online. Just don't bog things down with unnecessary detail, and remember – and I'm risking teaching you to suck eggs here – character lies at the heart of every good story. It's the people you create and then plunge into hell and high water who are the ones the readers buy your books to read about. You certainly won't need to do any research there.

But look, if there's something you really think you need to know about the police process, and you can't find any reference to it on the internet, or in a library, or anywhere like that, the solution is still simple.

Ask a policeman.

The Method and the Effect: Conjuring the Impossible Crime

Tom Mead

i.

The Paris night is racked by hellish screams. Following the sound, would-be rescuers flock to a nondescript house. They break open the door, they climb the staircase all the way to the fourth floor, to the source of those dreadful cries of terror. And they are confronted with another locked door.

Breaking down this door (finding its key still in the lock on the inside), they discover a scene of truly shocking, bloody horror. But the atrocity in that house in the Rue Morgue – the gruesome fates of Madame L'Espanaye and her daughter Camille – is magnified by the fact there was no conceivable way that the killer could have got in or out of the impenetrable room on the fourth floor…

Attempts to define the 'locked-room mystery' often (and wrongly) conflate it with the more common 'closed-circle mystery'. The latter term refers to a classic whodunit setup where a detective must identify a criminal from a 'closed circle' of suspects. What distinguishes the locked room from this other concept is an element of *impossibility*. Indeed, I tend to use 'locked-room mystery' as a synonym for 'impossible crime'. Essentially, it refers to a specialised subgenre of the vintage-style puzzle mystery in which a crime is committed under circumstances which appear to be physically impossible – what John Dickson Carr aptly terms 'the thing that can't happen but does happen'.[1]

With that in mind, impossible crime tales require particular meticulousness in their construction. They are, as Otto Penzler puts it, 'the ultimate manifestation of the cerebral detective story [which] fascinates the reader in precisely the same way that a magician is able to bring wonderment to his audience'.[2] The association between magic and impossible crime is decidedly apropos; both involve the mystification of an audience by a lone performer. Likewise, both are designed to evoke particularly intense emotions in their respective audiences. As Kingsley Amis puts it in his 1981 profile of John Dickson Carr, 'an almost painful curiosity' pervades.[3] The audience is drawn in by the demonstration of the impossible; a turning upside-down of one's perception of the world. But where the two art forms differ is in the resolution. Unlike a stage illusionist's audience,

---

[1] Carr, John Dickson, 'The Grandest Game in the World' in *The Door to Doom, and Other Detections* (Harper & Row, 1980) (Essay originally published 1963).

[2] Penzler, Otto, 'Introduction' in Penzler, Otto, (ed.), *The Black Lizard Big Book of Locked-Room Mysteries* (Vintage Crime/Black Lizard, 2014) p.xiii.

[3] Amis, Kingsley, *Times Literary Supplement*, 6 June 1981.

readers of impossible crime tales are 'looking for deliverance from the incredible'.[4] This ultimately manifests via a logical solution wherein rationality is restored.

Early examples of mystery tales featuring impossibilities include E.T.A. Hoffmann's 'Mademoiselle de Scuderi' (1819) and J. Sheridan Le Fanu's 'A Passage in the Secret History of an Irish Countess' (1838), but the first to combine the impossible problem *and* the detective story is Edgar Allan Poe's 'The Murders in the Rue Morgue' (1841), from which I appropriated the scenario for the opening of this chapter.

Indeed, detective fiction as we understand it would almost certainly not exist without Poe's tale. As Gothic fiction, it is a triumph – Grand Guignol in the most visceral sense of the term. And as mystery fiction, it is an essential milestone. During the nineteenth century, the impact of Poe's innovations was felt throughout the literary landscape, yielding several notable tales of seemingly supernatural phenomena resolved via ingenious earthly means. Prominent examples include Wilkie Collins's 'A Terribly Strange Bed' (1852) and Israel Zangwill's *The Big Bow Mystery* (1892), an unjustly forgotten title.

And reinforcing the association with the Gothic, William Hope Hodgson incorporated impossible crime elements into some of his stories featuring the enigmatic Carnacki, the Ghost-Finder. Carnacki is an 'occult detective', a series character whose investigations of unexplained phenomena frequently lead him into the realm of the uncanny. However, several tales in which he features do not involve anything otherworldly at all, but

---
4   Ibid.

rather earthly crimes disguised as the work of ghosts, curses and the like. A perfect example would be 'The Thing Invisible' (1912), in which a cursed dagger seems to seek out victims of its own accord in a haunted chapel. Here, the explanation is not in fact supernatural, but relies on an ingenious yet wholly human gimmick.

Other seminal works from this era include Jacques Futrelle's 'The Problem of Cell 13' (1905). This story is notable for the originality and ingenuity of its solution, but also for the fact that it's not an 'impossible crime' at all. Rather, Futrelle's master detective Professor Augustus S.F.X. van Dusen is challenged to escape from an impermeable cell – which, of course, he does. So there is a puzzle, a 'locked-room mystery' in a literal sense, but there is no crime. The story is a perfectly formed gem – the work of a formidable talent. Futrelle's life was cut tragically short in 1912 when he was killed in the *Titanic* disaster at the age of thirty-seven. Reading 'Cell 13', it is poignant to imagine what adventures his marvellous 'Thinking Machine' van Dusen might have undertaken if he had lived.

Likewise, Gaston Leroux's *The Mystery of the Yellow Room* (1907) is a pivotal early work – indeed, the aforementioned master of the locked-room mystery, John Dickson Carr, called it his favourite detective story. Its brilliance lies in the ultimate deceptive simplicity of its solution – something writers of impossible crimes have been striving for ever since.

Meanwhile, Arthur Conan Doyle's Sherlock Holmes tales essentially codified Poe's components of the detective story by placing emphasis on *how* mysteries were solved; focusing on the detection and thought processes of the detective – what Poe termed 'ratiocination'. Conan Doyle also created a couple of impossible crimes into the bargain: 'The Adventure of the Empty House' (1903) and his own favourite Holmes tale, 'The Adventure of the Speckled Band' (1892). This focus on mental acuity helped to pave the way for the so-called Golden Age of detective fiction, the decades between the world wars during which the cleverness of the detection and the cleverness of the puzzle assumed equal importance.

Numerous Golden Age practitioners have presented their 'rules' for crafting mysteries – with varying degrees of seriousness. Indeed, the famous credos of both Ronald Knox and S.S. Van Dine are certainly satiric in tone. But at their heart, they encompass the serious notion of playing fair with the reader; of ensuring that all clues and details necessary to solve the puzzle are present in the text. Hidden in plain sight, if you like.

As a writer, this may at first seem as though you are restricting yourself unnecessarily. But the perverse appeal of writing impossible crimes lies in not only playing by the rules but *embracing* them and the delicious challenge they present. They force you to be inventive, and stimulate the imagination in startling ways.

Indeed, there is a tendency to one-upmanship among the impossible crime crowd which can be seen throughout the Golden Age. It manifests in a need to devise the most bizarre impossible problem which nonetheless features a rational solution. Though the 'locked room' is an effective metaphor, it is by no means the only species of impossibility – there are plenty of variations on this overarching theme.

For instance, the impossible alibi is a marvellously technical construction pioneered by the likes of Freeman Wills Crofts. He uses it to great effect in *The Starvel Hollow Tragedy* (1927), among numerous others wherein a killer seems to have been in two places at once. As such, this 'locked room' is one of time rather than space. Meanwhile, Helen McCloy's magnificent *Through a Glass Darkly* (1950) returns to the realm of the uncanny with a novel in which the appearance of a doppelganger heralds impending death. Edmund Crispin's *The Moving Toyshop* (1946) does exactly what its title implies: a whole shop vanishes into thin air. Christianna Brand's *Death of Jezebel* (1948) is a superb achievement in which a murder takes place on stage in full view of an audience – and yet the killer's identity is a mystery. *Into Thin Air* (1928) by Horatio Winslow and Leslie Quirk presents us with a master criminal whose fingerprints appear at a crime scene months after his death. These are all variations on that same formula: a criminal achieving the impossible.

So what's the secret? How do these authors pull it off? To me, it is their focus on the reader. I would argue that such writers are more acutely aware of the psychology of their readers than in any other genre. Because the construction of a fair-play puzzle with a satisfying solution relies on an understanding of the gaps in our perception of the world, and the knowledge of how to exploit them.

ii.

At its most basic, my understanding of cognitive gaps comes from the work of the neurologist and author Oliver Sacks. As he puts it, 'we see with the eyes, but we see with the brain as well'.[5] It is the way in which our brain computes external stimuli that structures our understanding of the world. In Sacks's words: 'Every act of perception, is to some degree an act of creation, and every act of memory is to some degree an act of imagination.'[6]

Oliver Sacks's studies of abnormal brain injuries produced some remarkable (and thrillingly readable) accounts of extraordinary behaviours and symptoms which demonstrate the different functions of the brain. In effect, the lesson of his wonderful work is how *fragile* our perception of the world actually is, and how susceptible to manipulation. After all, the hand is most certainly *not* quicker than the eye; it is when the eye is looking in the wrong direction that the hand performs the trick. This brings us back to my favourite analogy for impossible crime: stage magic.

Sleights of Mind: What the Neuroscience of Magic Reveals about Our Everyday Deceptions (2010) by Stephen Macknik and Susana Martinez-Conde was recommended to me by Gigi Pandian – herself a devotee of the locked room, and author of an entertaining series of 'gothic cozies', the Secret Staircase

---

[5] Sacks, Oliver, 'What hallucination reveals about our minds' (TED Talk, 2009).

[6] Sacks, Oliver, *Musicophilia: Tales of Music and the Brain* (Pan Macmillan, 2011) p.127.

mysteries. It has very swiftly become one of my go-to resources. The book is a study of 'the neuroscience of magic', in other words, an examination of how different illusions 'work' on the human brain. Essentially, it's a guidebook on how to exploit those gaps in our perception. To me, this is the very heart of a successful impossible crime tale.

Generally speaking, Macknik and Martinez-Conde observe that 'humans have a hardwired process of attention and awareness that is hackable'.[7] Thus, if the mystery writer understands this process, they may be able to circumvent it. In the realm of magic, 'success relies on the magician's skill in diverting your attention away from the method and toward the magical effect'.[8] This is also true of impossible crime, and both rely on exploiting the everyday neurological processes which control 'attention, memory, and causal inference'.[9]

Sleights of Mind examines numerous methods for achieving this in depth; indeed, there are far too many to list here. But a useful example is that of 'source confusion'[10] – the brain's inability to distinguish between events which were directly observed and those which were *reported* by somebody else. When crafting a cast of characters with conflicting statements and alibis, this can be particularly useful. Indeed, John Dickson

---

7   Macknik, Stephen and Martinez-Conde, Susana, with Blakeslee, Sandra, *Sleights of Mind: What the Neuroscience of Magic Reveals about Our Everyday Deceptions* (Profile Books, 2010) p.6.

8   Ibid, p.66.

9   Ibid, p..59.

10 Ibid, p.118.

Carr makes tacit acknowledgement of this in his celebrated essay 'The Grandest Game in the World' when he observes that 'it is not at all necessary to mislead the reader. Merely state your evidence, and the reader will mislead himself.'[11]

In both magic and impossible crime, when we see something that defies our established perception of the world, it creates a kind of cognitive disconnect. It troubles us because we know that it should not be. The key difference between magic and mystery is that in magic it is crucial that the cognitive conflict is left unresolved. In mystery, it's crucial that it *is* resolved. The satisfaction comes from having one's concept of reality turned inside out by the demonstration of phenomena that is quantitatively impossible, only for prosaic, *real* reality to be reasserted via the unravelling of the mystery and the dispelling of the illusion.

There is something incredibly comforting and cathartic about seeing a pattern emerge from chaos before our eyes. It is human nature to seek patterns where there are none – take, for instance, the pareidolic phenomenon of perceiving faces in the clouds – and when we reach the end of a well-written puzzle mystery, the effect should be of all the seemingly superfluous details and bizarre happenings suddenly clicking neatly into place. As Carr puts it, 'each small detail glitters now with an effectiveness it should have had, and would have had, if the

---

[11] Carr, John Dickson, 'The Grandest Game in the World' in *The Door to Doom, and Other Detections* (Harper & Row, 1980) (Essay originally published 1963).

story had been written straightforwardly'.[12] And then, 'when… we find ourselves flumdiddled by some master stroke of ingenuity which has turned our suspicions legitimately in the wrong direction, we can only salute the author and close the book with a kind of admiring curse.'[13]

When I am plotting out the sequence of events for a locked-room mystery, I tend to construct two parallel timelines, consisting of *what the reader* thinks *happened* and *what actually happened*. Observing where these twin timelines diverge and converge is an interesting exercise in itself, and helps enormously with the creation of suspense, the planting of clues, and the development of characters. To my mind, it is also a reflection of those two key principles of prestidigitation: the method and the effect. One timeline reflects the method for the trick; the sleight-of-hand under the audience's nose. The other is the perceived effect: a seemingly impossible phenomenon which is in fact the result of deception.

As such, the impossible crime story relies on a close psychological bond between writer and reader – as does magic. The non-fiction study *Magic in Theory: An Introduction to the Theoretical and Psychological Elements of Conjuring* (1999) contains the observation that 'a spectator who thinks he knows how magic works can be, in some ways, easier to fool'.[14] This is also true of mystery readers, and nobody understood this better

---

12 Ibid.

13 Ibid.

14 Lamont, Peter and Wiseman, Richard, *Magic in Theory: An Introduction to the Theoretical and Psychological Elements of Conjuring* (University of Hertfordshire Press, 1999), p.14.

than the most brilliant and innovative exponent of the genre: the aforementioned John Dickson Carr.

Born in Uniontown, Pennsylvania, in 1906, Carr as a young man was enthralled by both magic and the gothic. As such he is part of a literary lineage that may be traced all the way back to Poe. A *New Yorker* profile of Carr which appeared in 1951 makes this very comparison, noting that Carr and Poe shared inner worlds of 'umbrageous fantasia'.[15] They were both drawn to 'the refined grotesqueries of an older civilisation'[16] – namely, Europe. Unlike Poe, though, Carr actually made it to Europe. He studied in France, which inspired his early mysteries, then subsequently hit his stride when he came to England at the height of the Golden Age.

Carr created four series detectives: Fell, Sir Henry Merrivale ('H.M.'), Henri Bencolin, and Colonel March. Both Fell and H.M. enjoyed particularly lengthy careers, with most of their tales featuring some form of impossible crime. But the one I am going to focus on here is a Fell novel, *The Hollow Man* (1935). This book is often discussed as Carr's masterpiece – to the point where Carr scholars are sick of talking about it – but the impact this book had on me was enormous. To me, that was the book that confirmed its author as the master of his craft. But it was also the book that set me off on my own creative path. I wanted to give readers the same experience that *I* had enjoyed in Carr's work; to recapture that magic, if you like.

One of the book's most notable features is a chapter in which

---

15 Taylor, Robert Lewis, *New Yorker*, 8 September 1951.

16 Ibid.

Fell seems to step outside the narrative and address the reader directly, delivering his now-famous 'locked-room lecture'. The true conceptual magnificence of the locked-room lecture is not immediately apparent on first reading. It reads, in fact, as a comprehensive list of solutions that other writers had previously devised for the conventional locked-room problem. It's a showcase for Carr's wide reading in the genre and his imagination. There is also considerable audacity in his placing something like this at the heart of a mystery novel; a passage which gives away just about every trick of his duplicitous trade.

But there's more to it than that. By rights, the locked-room lecture ought to contain the solutions to the mysteries at the heart of *The Hollow Man*. Does it? That is a surprisingly difficult question to answer – and a testament to Carr's genius. It's pure showboating: it is the magician saying to his audience, 'See? There is nothing up my sleeve.' It's all part of the psychological game the maestro is playing. Here is sleight-of-hand within sleight-of-hand. Tricks within tricks. An astonishingly subtle and nuanced performance *disguised* as a brash gambit. By confronting us with the problem head-on, proposing all manner of solutions and then picking them apart one by one, he *wants* us to play along. To second guess him. The game is more fun that way.

Carr was an anglophile, and during the 1930s and '40s he was essentially adopted by the British mystery writing community, becoming one of its greatest luminaries. But in his love of the impossible, he was certainly not alone.

iii.

While John Dickson Carr was the locked-room mystery genre's most prolific and vocal exponent during the Golden Age, countless contemporaries and successors also tackled the problem. These diverse perspectives demonstrate the surprising versatility of the form.

Take Philip Macdonald, who, under the pseudonym 'Martin Porlock', created a bizarre impossible scenario in *The Mystery at Friar's Pardon* (1931): a victim is found *drowned* in a locked room, though there was no water present. In this same vein, Rupert Penny (a pseudonym used by Ernest Basil Charles Thornett) penned a string of dazzling and unusual puzzle mysteries, many impossible, between 1936 and 1941. They are amazingly complex and technical in their construction, which of course means they are not to every reader's taste, but they nonetheless boast a richness and originality to entertain the exacting connoisseur. For instance, *Sealed Room Murder* (1941) requires no fewer than seven (!) diagrams to explain the murderer's method.

Leo Bruce ploughs a more comic furrow in *A Case for Three Detectives* (1936), which introduces his recurring detective, the gruff village policeman Sergeant Beef, who proudly runs rings around the eponymous three, each of whom is a humorous caricature of a different Golden Age sleuth. Hercule Poirot, for instance, is here parodied as 'Amer Picon'. The locked-room problem is pleasing, but even more so are the three different (and false) solutions given by each of the sleuths before they are put in their place by Beef, who has known the correct answer all along. (And speaking of Poirot, the great Belgian himself is faced with a remarkably bloody locked-room problem in *Hercule Poirot's Christmas* (1938).)

Although Carr, an American, became most closely associated with the Golden Age in Britain, the impossible crime was certainly not a purely British phenomenon. Its appeal could be seen throughout Europe, with the likes of French authors Gaston Boca, Noel Vindry and Pierre Véry carving successful careers as specialists in the locked room.

In the US, 'Ellery Queen' was a pseudonym used by two cousins, Frederic Dannay and Manfred B. Lee. Between them, they produced some of the most startlingly brilliant puzzle mysteries of the twentieth century. The early novels in particular place a significant emphasis on the *form* of the detective novel, with most featuring a 'challenge to the reader' in which the reader is cordially informed that all the clues have now been revealed which they could possibly require in order to solve the mystery for themselves.

Not many of the Ellery Queen novels feature impossibilities, but those that do are especially notable. *The Chinese Orange Mystery* (1934) offers a truly brilliant puzzle, though it must be said that the locked room element is actually the weakest part of the book. *The King is Dead* (1952) came considerably later in the Queen canon, and is a deliriously experimental entry in the series. The locked-room trick here is incredibly elaborate, but the book itself somewhat controversial among Queen fans because of its off-the-wall bizarre elements. Personally, I love it. But I think Ellery Queen's greatest and most enduring achievement in the field of impossible crime is *The Door Between* (1937), a book which boasts great atmosphere and profound psychological insight.

Another American with a knack for locked rooms was Anthony Boucher (a pseudonym for William Anthony Parker White) – whose pen name lives on thanks to the annual 'Bouchercon' crime fiction event. He was a great Renaissance man of the genre; a critic and scholar, as well as an occasional author. Though his output of fiction was more sporadic than others', he was remarkably good at it, and his *Nine Times Nine* (1940) is a classic of the locked-room subgenre in which a nun named Sister Ursula plays amateur detective to bring down a sinister cult.

Clayton Rawson, meanwhile, was a personal friend of Carr, as well as one of the founders of the Mystery Writers of America and – crucially – a professional magician. His detective character was also a magician: The Great Merlini. The Merlini mysteries teem with brilliant literary sleights-of-hand, and they are crammed with wonderful details about the life of a professional illusionist. As you can imagine, many of the puzzles hinge on impossibilities, with the first book, *Death from a Top Hat* (1938), being perhaps the most acclaimed.

Similarly, Hake Talbot was a pseudonym used by the professional magician Henning Nelms. Talbot/Nelms wrote only two mysteries – *The Hangman's Handyman* (1942) and *Rim of the Pit* (1944) – both of which are triumphs of literary legerdemain that reflect their author's mastery of the real-life 'dark arts'.

Talbot is, of course, not the only one- or two-hit wonder from this period. Theodore Roscoe, for instance, wrote primarily for the pulp fiction market, but two of his novels, *Murder on the Way!* (1935) and *I'll Grind Their Bones* (1936), offer excellent locked rooms. Additionally, Bruce Elliott's *You'll Die Laughing* (1945) is utterly bizarre and (as far as I am aware) completely original in its solution. It's also notable because Elliott was yet another professional magician.

Likewise, Joel Townsley Rogers's *The Red Right Hand* (1945) is a bona fide masterpiece of suspense bordering on psychological terror, and while it is not *explicitly* an impossible crime it nonetheless conjures similar uncanny sensations in the reader as the boundaries of logic are breached. The same goes for Fredric Brown's *Night of the Jabberwock* (1950), though Brown did write more straightforward locked-room problems in such novels as *Death Has Many Doors* (1951), not to mention the bizarre (and brilliant) puzzles in his short fiction, including 'The Laughing Butcher' and 'The Spherical Ghoul'. Virgil Markham's *The Devil Drives* (1932), meanwhile, infuses its puzzle with doom-laden noir akin to *Nightmare Alley*.

Herbert Brean was a journalist whose sideline as a mystery author yielded several little-read but highly regarded titles. Of these, the first – *Wilders Walk Away* (1948) – is perhaps the best known, and sees young photographer Reynold Frame embroiled in the affairs of the mysterious Wilder family. Seemingly bewitched by supernatural forces, the Wilders have an eerie habit of disappearing in impossible circumstances – they simply 'walk away'. Their small New England town is so steeped in the mythology of their disappearances that it has produced a haunting nursery rhyme:

Other people die of mumps
Or general decay,
Of fevers, chills, or other ills,
But Wilders walk away.

Though this book is the most renowned, Brean wrote other, later gems, including *Hardly a Man is Now Alive* (1950) and *The Traces of Brillhart* (1960).

Though most of these works share an atmosphere of foreboding, the impossible crime is actually a surprisingly versatile beast. For instance, Alan Green's *What a Body!* (1949) is a humorous satire on the burgeoning self-help boom. In it, a health and fitness guru is killed in inexplicable circumstances. The light tone of this one makes the ingenuity of its solution all the more pleasing.

Outside of Europe and America, Japan also saw a boom in puzzle mysteries – particularly of the impossible variety – during the first half of the twentieth century. Among the leading lights of the *honkaku* ('orthodox') puzzle mystery was Edogawa Ranpo. The pseudonym is in fact a phonetic rendering of 'Edgar Allan Poe' ('Edoga-' = Edgar, '-wa Ranpo' = Allan Poe). Like Poe, Carr, and various others, his work is informed by a singularly macabre imagination. Take, for instance, 'The Human Chair', a short story in which a chairmaker fashions a sofa so perfect that he decides to hollow it out and live in it, unknown and undetected by the sofa's new owners. It's a kind of inverted locked-room scenario, designed to evoke psychological dread, as the unnamed assailant sneaks out of his strange hidey-hole under cover of darkness and engages in all manner of criminality. Ranpo's contemporaries included Tetsuya Ayakawa, Seishi Yokomizo and Keikichi Osaka, all of whom boasted incredibly dexterous imaginations and a flair for the surreal.

While this global Golden Age produced many, many excellent novels in the impossible crime genre, it's important not to neglect the short story form, which also had a lot to offer. Carr's 'The Wrong Problem', 'The House in Goblin Wood' and 'Blind Man's Hood' are masterpieces in miniature. Likewise, Clayton Rawson thrived in this particular area, with one of his Merlini stories – 'From Another World' – rivalling the maestro himself.

For all the complexities of the impossible problem, which make it a particularly challenging subject for short fiction, there are some who thrive within the constraints of the form. For instance, Joseph Commings's boisterous amateur sleuth Senator Brooks U. Banner appeared in a grand total of thirty-three tales, all of which feature some species of impossibility. Banner himself is essentially a caricature constituted entirely of eccentricities and outrageousness, rather like Carr's Sir Henry Merrivale. Indeed, 'Fingerprint Ghost' features a pleasing, Carr-inspired solution which was subsequently appropriated for the pilot episode of TV's *Jonathan Creek*. All the tales have something to offer, though 'The X Street Murders' and the non-series 'Bones for Davy Jones' are particular highlights. Fourteen of the Banner stories are collected in *Banner Deadlines* (2004), issued by the premier publisher of single-author mystery collections, Crippen & Landru.

Then there is Arthur Porges, whose wide reading and ingenuity led him to produce four series characters (Dr Joel Hoffmann, Ulysses Price Middlebie, Julian Morse Trowbridge, and Dr Cyriack Skinner Grey) and a range of brilliant puzzles. Indeed, his criminous brain was so multifariously cunning that he presented the same problem twice (in 'A Puzzle in Sand' and 'No Killer Has Wings'), with two entirely different solutions!

But as every professional writer knows, it is remarkably difficult to make a living solely from the production of short stories. And yet that's exactly what post-Golden Age great Edward D. Hoch did. Hoch wrote only a couple of novels in his lifetime, yet churned out short fiction at an astronomical rate, producing almost a thousand. He had numerous series characters with incredibly diverse backgrounds and personalities. Nick Velvet, for instance, was a professional thief. Captain Leopold was a cop. Sam Hawthorne was a small-town doctor in the first half of the twentieth century. Jeffery Rand was a British intelligence agent a la Le Carre's George Smiley. Simon Ark was a 2,000-year-old Coptic priest (or so he claimed). Hopefully this gives you an idea of the dizzying breadth of his imagination. The fact that most of his stories also feature impossible crimes and/or locked-room mysteries is positively awe-inspiring.

Indeed, Hoch's oeuvre reflects the sheer malleability of the impossible crime as a concept. It can be comic, sad, or chilling. It can be surreal, bizarre, outré, just as long as it establishes its own logical framework; its own set of 'rules'. This tendency can be observed in numerous post-Golden Age novels, too. For instance, *Too Many Magicians* (1966) by Randall Garrett is set in a world where magic of the fantastical variety is commonplace. This kind of genre-bending helped to keep the impossible crime alive during the post-war decades when puzzle mysteries were decidedly démodé.

Indeed, as with the Golden Age in British and American mystery fiction, *honkaku* fell out of favour in Japan during the aftermath of the Second World War. It took a whole new literary movement in the late 1970s and early '80s to revive it. This was the so-called 'shin-honkaku', or 'new orthodox', pioneered by the likes of Soji Shimada, Yukito Ayatsuji and Keigo Higashino, all of whose works are now steadily appearing in English. It has even infiltrated the worlds of manga and anime thanks to the likes of Gosho Aoyama's superb *Detective Conan* series.

During the 1970s and '80s, both British and American authors also helped to stimulate interest in the genre by incorporating it into more straightforward mysteries – and even police procedurals. William L. DeAndrea, for instance, was an author whose star burned bright but too briefly; between 1978 and his death in 1996 at age forty-four, he penned several series and won three Edgar Awards. His longest-running series was set in the world of television and featured amateur detective Matt Cobb, who solved a knotty impossible problem in *Killed on the Rocks* (1990). DeAndrea also paid homage to the Golden Age with his Nero Wolfe-inspired Niccolo Benedetti mysteries, of which he wrote only three, but which are perfectly plotted and while not exactly locked rooms, are certainly locked-room adjacent. DeAndrea also happened to be married to the author Orania Papazoglou, who wrote the excellent Gregor Demarkian mysteries under the name 'Jane Haddam'. Under her own name, though, she also penned a superb locked-room mystery called *Sweet, Savage Death* in 1985.

Bill Pronzini, meanwhile, faced his 'Nameless Detective' with excellent puzzles and several literal locked rooms in what was otherwise a noirish private eye series. The most prominent examples are *Hoodwink* (1981) and *Scattershot* (1982). Pronzini is in fact one of the most prolific locked-room authors of recent decades, and his non-series story 'The Arrowmont Prison Riddle' features an especially original trick. Pronzini's wife, Marcia Muller, is also an accomplished author whose novel *The Tree of Death* (1983) sees a murder in a locked museum. In recent years, she and Pronzini have begun an effective collaboration on a series of historical mysteries, many featuring impossibilities as well.

Likewise, Peter Lovesey is one of the UK's best and most prolific novelists. He manages to combine the police procedural with the puzzle mystery format, and imbue the whole thing with a sense of humour that is all-too-often lacking in contemporary crime. Though his impossible tales are comparatively few and far between, their quality is ample compensation. *Bloodhounds* (1996), the fourth in his Peter Diamond series, is one of the very best post-Golden Age impossible problems, and original too, for it features a corpse found on a locked canal barge. It is a marvellously self-aware work, with copious references to the maestro John Dickson Carr. And Lovesey presents a unique impossibility in 'The Amorous Corpse' – a robber dies during a hold-up at the same moment he was at home making love to his girlfriend. Talk about coitus interruptus!

THE METHOD AND THE EFFECT

For a genre that may at first seem staid and predictable, it is astonishing how diverse it can be. Perhaps that is why the impossible crime has attracted so many authors who are better known in the field of science fiction, specifically: Jack Vance, John Sladek and Isaac Asimov, all of whom produced thoroughly excellent locked rooms that combine bold flights of fancy with meticulous attention to detail. More recently, *The Real-Town Murders* (2017) by Adam Roberts is set in a dystopian future where advancements in (fictional) technology conspire to make an impossible problem *all the more* impossible.

Conversely, other authors have sought inspiration in the past, with Paul Doherty producing over a hundred historical mysteries. Though there are so many to choose from, *The Nightingale Gallery* (1991) and *The Mask of Ra* (1998) offer particularly delectable impossibilities set in Medieval England and Ancient Egypt, respectively.

It's also intriguing to note the flexibility the genre offers in terms of tone and style. Like the aforementioned Gigi Pandian, Victoria Dowd is a contemporary author who combines the recognisable tropes of 'cosy' crime with the locked-room mystery to excellent effect in her 'Smart Woman's Guide to Murder' series. So does Robert Thorogood, whose TV shows *Death in Paradise* and *Marlow Murder Club* have brought the locked room back into millions of homes and whose novels reflect a deep knowledge and appreciation for the genre.

Martin Edwards, meanwhile, incorporates impossible problems into his 1930s-set Rachel Savernake series at a heartening rate, with the newest title being *Sepulchre Street* (2023).

Similarly, the German author Rob Reef has done excellent work reinvigorating the vintage-style puzzle in his 'Stableford' series, though these have yet to appear in English.

At the same time, the self-publishing boom of recent years has given voice to numerous new and interesting exponents of the genre, including Hal White, whose *Mysteries of Reverend Dean* (2008) appears (lamentably) to be a one-off; James Scott Byrnside, whose Rowan Manory series is an excellent and underappreciated gem; while Jim Noy's *The Red Death Murders* (2022) brings the genre full circle, so to speak, by placing a bold locked-room plot in the world of Edgar Allan Poe's 'The Masque of the Red Death'.

But there is one last author who deserves a mention here. He is, after all, frequently cited as the natural successor to John Dickson Carr: Paul Halter. Halter's brilliance lies in his embrace of the surreal; the most bizarre aspects of Carr, with occasional dashes of Fredric Brown, Joel Townsley Rogers, Hake Talbot, and others. Though a Frenchman himself, most of his works are set in a fictionalised England – a land in thrall to legends, folklore, ghost stories. This 'heightening' of the setting and the characters facilitates the creation of more complex problems, it gives the author scope to take the story in startling new directions while still playing fair with readers. Case in point: *The Invisible Circle* (1996), a fascinating standalone which is steeped in Arthurian legend, yet contains a fair-play earthly solution to its puzzles.

Meanwhile, *The Demon of Dartmoor* (1993) features a stunning impossibility – a man pushed to his death by invisible forces – with a solution that is so dazzling in its simplicity that it really does call to mind Carr at his most devious. *The Crimson Fog* (1988) offers a murder *during* a magic show, and a conceit which is both wonderfully clever and wonderfully macabre. *The Picture from the Past* (1995) is a marvellous Borgesian web; *The Vampire Tree* (1996) is a gloriously grotesque exercise in Grand Guignol; and *The Seven Wonders of Crime* (1997) is, as the title implies, a startlingly ambitious work with no fewer than *seven* impossibilities. These brief descriptions ought to give you an idea of the fecundity of Paul Halter's imagination, and indeed the sheer dexterity of familiar locked-room tropes overall.

The preceding examples chart the development and diversification of the genre beyond its commonly perceived limitations, and the increasingly original and eccentric methods employed by a broad cross-section of authors in pursuit of the same tantalising effect. I am continually awed by Halter, Carr, Queen, and the many other authors I have discussed here. Indeed, I am not only fascinated by the astonishing effects themselves, but with *how* those effects are created.

The impossible mystery is the most challenging of all the diverse subgenres of crime fiction. But when it works, it works beautifully. It provides both reader and writer with the profound sensation of sanity being drawn from the depths of madness, like seeing a jigsaw assembled before their eyes, or hearing the comforting click of a key in a lock. It is a unique, subtle brand of magic, and there really is nothing else quite like it.

Spotlight on...
Sir Arthur Conan Doyle

The Problem of the Faithful Pastiche

Tim Major

I had been sitting motionless at my desk for innumerable minutes, having produced not a single scratch of pen upon paper. At the sound of a carriage pulling up in the street outside I rose and moved to the window, grateful for the interruption.

'Perhaps we will be occupied to-day after all,' I said. 'I suspect this carriage has brought us a client.'

Sherlock Holmes lay in a reclined position in his velvet armchair, one arm covering his eyes, every inch the Bohemian idle. Without changing his posture in the least, he said, 'Expectations are distinct from deductions, Watson. How many of our clients arrive in light gigs as opposed to broughams?'

I gazed at the two-wheeled carriage in the street below. 'Are you really able to identify it as a gig simply from the sound it produces?'

My friend did not reply. I watched on as the driver bent to retrieve something from beneath his seat, then alighted from the gig to approach our door.

'I note that he favours his left leg,' Holmes murmured.

'That's extraordinary!' I said as I saw that it was true. I had known Holmes to form deductions based on the sounds of footsteps on the stairs that lead to our rooms, but the degree of acuity required to determine a man's gait outside the building struck me as remarkable.

'Is there anything else you can tell me about the fellow?' I asked eagerly.

'He is no older than twenty-five. He is clean shaven.' Holmes hesitated, and I turned to see him cock his head as though listening intently. 'Furthermore, I understand he is carrying a covered wooden crate with utmost care.'

Now my amazement knew no bounds. All of these observations were indisputably true.

I rounded on Holmes to demand, 'How can you possibly have—'

Holmes swung his legs from the chair and rose in a single movement. At the very same moment, the doorbell rang downstairs. He placed a hand on my shoulder, then turned to await Mrs Hudson, who would soon escort our visitor to our door.

'We will take this up later,' he said. 'For now, let us see if our expectations are to be met.'

Mounting expectations

Long before he achieved worldwide success, Arthur Conan Doyle was acutely aware that his intended readers had particular expectations – and yet he failed to anticipate them.

After he completed *A Study in Scarlet* in April 1886, he sent it directly to James Payn, editor of *The Cornhill Magazine*, who declared it 'capital' but concluded that it was 'too long – and too short'. That is, it was too short to be serialised and too long to be published in a single issue. The chief editor of Ward, Lock & Co gave the manuscript to his wife to read, who reported, 'This man is a born novelist! It will be a great success!' yet while the 1887 edition of *Beeton's Christmas Annual* that contained *A Study in Scarlet* sold out, Sherlock Holmes was yet to have definitively 'arrived' in the public consciousness. The next Holmes novel, *The Sign of Four*, appeared in English and American editions of *Lippincott's* in February 1890, but even when it was published in book form later that year it attracted few reviews and little success.

The factor that would alter Conan Doyle's fortunes – by better fulfilling the expectations of a readership in waiting – was a change of format. Between April and August 1891, he sent six Holmes short stories to a new publication, *The Strand*, and all of them were published that year. The overwhelming public response led *The Strand*'s editor to beg Conan Doyle for more. He refused at first, but finally relented, having negotiated a payment of £50 per story, regardless of length. Once these additional six stories had been delivered, Conan Doyle wrote to his mother to confess that he had considered killing his detective in the twelfth tale, stating that Holmes 'takes my mind from better things'.[1] In February 1892, he asked for an astounding £1,000 to write another twelve Holmes stories, secretly hoping the offer would be refused. It was accepted.

But Conan Doyle was determined to have his way. After an 1893 visit to the Reichenbach Falls in Switzerland, he killed Sherlock Holmes.

No doubt the aftermath of the publication of 'The Final Problem' was when Conan Doyle appreciated just how important a public figure Holmes had become. He had considered the killing of his character a personal decision, but the outcry from his readership was intense. A Holmes story raised circulation of *The Strand* by 100,000 copies, and upon Holmes's death 20,000 subscriptions were cancelled. Readers wore black bands of mourning, and Conan Doyle received accusatory letters. He would eventually relent, first inserting Holmes into his Gothic 'creeper', *The Hound of the Baskervilles*, set in a period predating Holmes's death, and finally reviving the detective to resume short-story publications from 1903 onwards.

Perhaps Holmes might have thrived even if Conan Doyle hadn't bowed to his readers' expectations. By the time the great detective was officially returned to life, Holmes had already

---

[1] Lellenberg, Jon, Daniel Stashower & Charles Foley (eds), *Arthur Conan Doyle: A Life in Letters* (HarperPress, 2007) p.300.

established an existence apart from his creator, beginning in earnest in 1899 when William Gillette's play *Sherlock Holmes* premiered at the Garrick Theatre in New York City, starring Gillette himself. Significantly, it was Gillette who first had Holmes utter the phrase, 'Elementary, my dear Watson.' Conan Doyle had been generous in allowing latitude to develop the character: when Gillette asked, 'May I marry Sherlock Holmes?' Conan Doyle replied, 'You may marry him, murder him, or do anything you like with him.'[2]

Even Conan Doyle himself wasn't above producing non-canonical Holmes tales. In 1896, three years after the 'death' of Holmes, his two-page story 'The Field Bazaar' appeared in the magazine of the student council of the University of Edinburgh, produced for an event to raise money for a cricket pavilion. The story features a familiar example of Holmes's deductive prowess in a scene within 221b Baker Street, but what is notable is its metatextual content: Holmes deduces that Watson has received a letter asking him for help with the Edinburgh University bazaar, concluding, 'the particular help which you have been asked to give was that you should write in their album, and that you have already made up your mind that the present incident will be the subject of your article.'[3] Similarly parodic is Conan Doyle's 503-word story of 1924, 'How Watson Learned the Trick', in which Watson tries and

---

2   Orel, Harold, *Critical Essays on Sir Arthur Conan Doyle* (G. K. Hall & Co., 1992) p.5.

3   Conan Doyle, Arthur, 'The Field Bazaar', in *The Student* (Edinburgh University, 1896).

fails to ape his friend's deductive processes. This story was a particularly unusual brand of spin-off merchandising, written by hand in a book measuring 3.75cm by 3.15cm, for inclusion in the miniature library of Queen Mary's dolls' house. There were other unexploited opportunities, too: Conan Doyle was reportedly amenable to an American publisher's idea of writing a biography of Dr Watson in lieu of additional 'straight' Holmes tales.

From these early deviations Holmes grew in confidence, and now he can be found in countless films, stories, comics, novels and videogames. Readers' mental images of the great detective are likely to have been formed by a hotch-potch of portrayals and pop-culture references. My own children know the character primarily from the silhouettes on the spines of the books on my shelf, a Holmes-themed escape-room game, and the 2018 animated film *Sherlock Gnomes*, in which the great detective is a ceramic garden ornament. Others may visualise Basil Rathbone, or Jeremy Brett, or Benedict Cumberbatch, or other portrayals from film and TV. Even during the initial reception of Conan Doyle's first short stories in *The Strand*, the accompanying illustrations by Sidney Paget were central to readers' image of the detective. The curved meerschaum pipe, deerstalker and ever-present magnifying glass were Paget's inventions, tolerated by Conan Doyle. The fact that *The Strand*'s publishers had intended for the letter of commission to be sent to Paget's younger brother, Walter, demonstrates how close the world came to a very different image of the character.

What is a 'faithful' Holmes novel?

When I was asked by my publisher to write a Sherlock Holmes novel in the style of Conan Doyle, my first response was to panic. Most writers grapple with imposter syndrome, a lack of faith that their work is of worth. But this novel was to be a faithful pastiche of the original stories – that is, I would be voluntarily behaving as an imposter from the off.

I found myself dwelling not on Conan Doyle, but on Pierre Menard, the fictional author who appears in Jorge Luis Borges' short story 'Pierre Menard, Author of the *Quixote*'. The story is framed as an academic article about Menard's work, focusing on his attempt to write Cervantes' *Don Quixote* – but a perfectly faithful *Quixote* rather than a retelling:

> He did not want to compose another *Quixote*, which is easy – but *the Quixote itself*. Needless to say, he never contemplated a mechanical transcription of the original; he did not propose to copy it. His admirable ambition was to produce a few pages which would coincide – word for word and line for line – with those of Miguel de Cervantes.[4]

Borges' darkly funny account details Menard's attempts to become Cervantes in order to attempt his act of creation: he learns Spanish, converts to Catholicism, attempts to forget the history of the world post-1602. But having abandoned this

---
4   Borges, Jorge Luis, *Labyrinths* (Penguin, 1970) p.65.

approach and yet having painstakingly produced two chapters of *Don Quixote* – 'word for word and line for line' – the essay concludes that Menard's work is more valuable than Cervantes' because none of the material would come naturally to him as it would to its original author.

While Borges takes the idea of channelling an earlier work to an absurd extreme, Menard's effort echoes Margaret A. Rose's description of pastiche as 'literary forgery', albeit without necessarily having the intention to hoax.[5] Rose notes that a pastiche or parody must 'take into account the role of the expectations of the reader in the actual reception of the work'[6] – that is, no pastiche can be written without consideration of not only the works that have come before, but also readers' responses to those works. In short, it all comes back to expectations. Readers have them, and writers must anticipate them.

In order to predict the expectations of the reader, the author must bear in mind who this imagined recipient of the text may be, referred to by Wolfgang Iser as the 'implied reader'.[7] All novels are in dialogue not only with the 'implied reader' but with earlier literary works, particularly within specific genres. An author of mystery stories may assume that readers are familiar with the most common literary conventions related to detection and deduction. When writing my own novels, I tend to think about a 'contract' with the reader. I'm aware

---

5   Rose, Margaret A., *Parody//Meta-Fiction* (Croom Helm, 1979) p.43.

6   Ibid., p.114.

7   Iser, Wolfgang, *The Implied Reader* (Johns Hopkins University Press, 1974). The term 'implicit reader' is used in some translations.

that hundreds of thousands of books are published in the UK alone each year, and that I am writing for an 'implied reader' who has chosen to read my novel over others, based on certain expectations. These may be a result of, for example, the cover image, the back-cover blurb or reviews, all of which may suggest a certain flavour of reading experience. So, any surprises contained within the novel must be balanced with reassurances. The reader must be brought on board in the first place, if they're to enjoy the journey.

In the case of the commissioned Sherlock Holmes novel, I was not being asked, like Pierre Menard, to reproduce Conan Doyle's work afresh, or to become Conan Doyle to write my novel. I was simply to produce a novel in the same spirit as the canonical tales, for modern readers.

A perfectly reasonable request. But I asked myself again and again: *What is a 'faithful' Holmes novel?*

The Holmesian canon contains fifty-six short stories and four novels. Every one of these tales contain material rich for development as pastiche: plot points, expressions of character, fleeting comments. As my first task was to develop a plot synopsis for approval by my publisher, in my rereading I was drawn initially to the novels, in the hope of finding a structural template on which to model my own.

There was no template to be found. I was being commissioned to write a novel of 70,000 words, nowadays a more or less standard length in terms of the expectations (that word again!) of a modern genre publisher. An examination of the word counts of Conan Doyle's novels evokes *Cornhill Magazine* editor James Payn's assessment of the first novel being 'too long – and too short': *A Study in Scarlet* and *The Sign of Four* each run to 43,000 words, *The Hound of the Baskervilles* 59,000 words, and *The Valley of Fear* 57,000 words. The longer extents of the latter novels are somewhat misleading given that Holmes is absent for long portions of *The Hound of the Baskervilles*, and *The Valley of Fear* features an extensive flashback to events leading up to the central murder, in which neither Holmes nor Watson appear. Given that almost all of the short stories in the canon feature Holmes in a central role, it's perhaps surprising that there is no example of a 'full-length' Holmes novel in which that characteristic is fulfilled. How, then, ought a pastiche-writer to resolve this issue, if Conan Doyle either couldn't achieve it, or chose not to attempt to do so?

All the same, few modern readers are likely to question the wisdom of producing a new Sherlock Holmes novel. In the UK, Sherlock Holmes as a character, and the entirety of the canon, has been in the public domain since 2000, a fact exploited by a great number of authors eager to add to the great detective's casebook.[8] Yet I think this popular acceptance indicates a sort of shared false memory. We have all consumed so much Sherlockian fiction across all media that the idea that Conan Doyle himself never took the great detective on a 'full-length' adventure may

---

8   Publication of new Holmes tales has been complicated by US copyright; until 2023, only the canonical works up to 1923 could be drawn upon freely in the US. In 2022, the estate of Arthur Conan Doyle brought a case against Netflix for the depiction of the great detective in *Enola Holmes*, stating that a Sherlock Holmes capable of 'human connection and empathy' belonged to the later stories in the canon. The case was eventually dismissed.

seem absurd. In order to take into account the expectations of the reader, a pastiche-writer must navigate those *false* memories and assumptions. I was to produce a novel faithful to canonical Sherlock Holmes novels that, in fact, never existed.

Hallmarks of the canon

My attention shifted from structure to plots. Thankfully, Conan Doyle himself provided guidance as to the type of mysteries that would be appropriate. In an interview published in *Tit-Bits* magazine in 1900, he noted that before commencing work on *A Study in Scarlet* he read a number of detective stories, and concluded that 'they one and all filled me with dissatisfaction and a sort of feeling how much more interesting they might be made if one could show the man deserved his victory over the criminal or the mystery he was called upon to solve.'[9] His dissatisfaction related to the centrality of coincidence within the plots: 'They struck me as not a fair way of playing the game, because the detective ought really to depend for his success on something in his own mind and not on merely adventitious circumstances, which do not, by any means, always occur in real life.'[10]

This, then, was Conan Doyle's great innovation: a detective whose achievements were the result of his mental capacity. Yet the insistence that the detective must apply his mind to reach

---

9 Conan Doyle, Arthur, 'A Gaudy Death: Conan Doyle Tells the True Story of Sherlock Holmes's End', *Tit-Bits* (George Newnes Ltd., 1900).

10 Ibid.

the solution of the mystery doesn't mean that the reader can be expected to do likewise. In Conan Doyle's own words: 'The first thing is to get your idea. Having got that key idea one's next task is to conceal it and lay emphasis upon everything which can make for a different explanation.'[11] A contrasting approach, the so-called 'fair-play' rules of detective fiction, can be traced back to Ronald Knox's 1928 'Ten Commandments' of plot devices, adherence to which produced mysteries solvable before the final reveal, using clues seeded throughout the novel. One crucial commandment is: 'The detective must not light on any clues which are not instantly produced for the inspection of the reader.'[12] Holmes, on the other hand, is more than happy to operate *unfairly* by conducting investigations in secret, hiding his clues and his mental processes from both Watson and the reader.

This characteristic unfairness is likely to have registered in the public consciousness. Most adaptations portray Sherlock Holmes as vastly more intelligent than Watson and the layperson, and most of their plots permit Holmes to have his secrets. In many screen versions, emphasis is placed on adventure rather than detection, and the revelation of the mystery is more akin to the flourish of a magician than the sober conclusion of a detective. Other adaptations offer insights into Holmes's methods, creating visual representations of Holmes's 'brain-attic' (to which he alludes in *A Study in Scarlet*, having populated this mental

---

11   Conan Doyle, Arthur, *Memories and Adventures* (Little, Brown, 1924), p.102.

12   Knox, Ronald, *The Best English Detective Stories of 1928* (Horace Liverlight, 1929), Introduction, p.xi.

space with crucial information relating to human behaviour but nothing, for example, about the Solar System). These include the complex, interwoven images associating disparate clues in Benoit Dahan's and Cyril Lieron's graphic novel *Inside the Mind of Sherlock Holmes*, and the superimposed text and representational 'mind palace' depicted during deductive sequences in the BBC TV series *Sherlock*.[13] These insights often serve to humanise a character whom Conan Doyle described in his autobiography as a 'calculating machine', before adding a potential warning for pastiche-writers: 'and anything you add to that simply weakens the effect'.[14]

Holmes as a character may be firmly established in the minds of the general public, but his adventures are less ingrained and misconceptions about them are rife. A case in point: in many of the canonical stories Sherlock Holmes does not contribute to the capture of criminals. As Martin Edwards notes of the first batch of stories collected in *The Adventures of Sherlock Holmes*, 'criminals elude Holmes in one quarter of the cases in the book. He contemplates breaking the law more than once, and twice he lets the culprit go free.'[15] Similarly, Christopher Clausen points out that 'justice, not the defense of the existing order, is Holmes's ostensible aim in nearly all of the stories'.[16]

---

13 Videogames are a rare instance where the viewpoint is generally aligned to Holmes rather than Watson, and these treatments often struggle with the need to portray Holmes as preternaturally intelligent and yet also guided entirely by the player.

14 Conan Doyle, *Memories and Adventures*, p.103.

15 Edwards, Martin, *The Life of Crime* (Collins Crime Club, 2022), p.61.

16 Clausen, Christopher, 'Sherlock Holmes, Order, and the Late-Victorian

That justice is often expressed privately, with Holmes extracting a confession from the guilty party but failing to hand them over to the police. If order is restored, it is usually in terms of personal relationships and the application of a moral, rather than legal, sense of right and wrong. While readers may expect sermonising from, say, G.K. Chesterton's amateur detective Father Brown, the conclusion offered by Holmes at the end of 'The Creeping Man' may surprise anyone primarily familiar with pop-culture portrayals of the character: 'When one tries to rise above Nature one is liable to fall below it. The highest type of man may revert to the animal if he leaves the straight road of destiny.'[17]

My own ability to recall the plot of novels or films is embarrassingly limited. I tend to retain only flashes of plot details, or particular scenes. For example, I remember the *sense* of trickery in 'The Red-Headed League', but not the exact nature of the trick. I remember the confusion inspired by the word *RACHE* being daubed on the wall in *A Study in Scarlet* – is it the German word for 'revenge', or an unfinished 'Rachel'? – but the truth of the matter is hazy. Perhaps other readers suffer from the same forgetfulness, to a greater or lesser extent, and so writing for the 'implied reader' involves predicting what has been forgotten and what has been retained. In order to reproduce the *feel* of the stories, relatively minor hallmarks of the canon seem to me more crucial than echoing the broader narratives of the

---

Mind', in Orel, p.76.

17 Conan Doyle, Arthur, 'The Adventure of the Creeping Man', in *The Case-Book of Sherlock Holmes*, p.183.

original tales. Examples of these touchstones include minor scenes within 221b Baker Street in which Holmes displays his deductive prowess to Watson to solve a trivial matter unconnected to any crime, or Holmes's digressions on subjects unrelated to the task at hand, or references to cases as yet undocumented by Watson.

Another consideration is how closely to hew to the preoccupations of the original stories. While Holmes's aim may be 'justice, not the defense of the existing order', a great deal of his deductions are reliant upon his subject's adherence to the class structure of the day in terms of, for example, clothes, social circles and behaviour. Kim Herzinger notes that neither Holmes nor Conan Doyle display any interest in the poverty that has given rise to the urchins that populate the Baker Street Irregulars;[18] that social and political context is as unimportant to Holmes as planetary orbits. There are other pertinent issues that Holmes ignores or believes incorrectly. He makes no use of fingerprint identification, even though the practice was known at the time of writing. He is convinced that heredity has a substantial influence on criminal psychology. Importantly – in terms of posing an obstacle to modern readers – he harbours prejudices against particular social classes, races, and women. To what degree should a 'faithful' Holmes pastiche agree with his pronouncement in *The Sign of Four* that 'Women are never to be entirely trusted – not the best of them'?[19]

---

18   Herzinger, Kim, 'Inside and Outside Sherlock Holmes: A Rhapsody', in Orel, p.111.

19   Conan Doyle, Arthur, *The Sign of Four*, p.83.

In my three Sherlock Holmes pastiche novels I have felt free to include women in prominent roles. The client in *The Back to Front Murder* is Abigail Moone, who is not only complex and forthright, but also independent, having generated sizable wealth. In my third Holmes novel, *The Twelve Thefts of Christmas*, I not only return Irene Adler[20] to the stage (literally and figuratively), but also give Mary Watson and Mrs Hudson central roles. While these decisions are far from in keeping with Conan Doyle's work, they allowed me to explore interesting new territory by having Holmes butt up against his own prejudices.

My character Abigail Moone also allowed examination of an aspect that has little emphasis in the canon: Watson as a writer. Moone has made her fortune as an author (using a male pseudonym), and Watson is preoccupied by the idea that not only is she a better writer than himself, but that she might be more suited than him to the role of biographer of Sherlock Holmes, a possibility that seems to me ripe for examination.

With a different biographer, the accounts of Holmes's cases would be immeasurably different, as everything we know about Sherlock Holmes is relayed to us by Watson. Occasionally, he confesses that his accounts are far from verbatim, as in 'The Illustrious Client', when he notes that Holmes's 'hard, dry statement needs some little editing to soften it into the terms of real life'.[21] Furthermore, the reader's

---

20   The adventuress seen only in 'A Scandal in Bohemia' whose cunningness attracts Holmes's attention: 'To Sherlock Holmes she is always *the* woman'.

21   Conan Doyle, Arthur, 'The Adventure of the Illustrious Client', in *The Case-Book of Sherlock Holmes*, p.21.

enjoyment of any given case is to a large extent dictated by Watson's stylistic and narrative decisions. While the Holmes stories are presented in the past tense, Peter V. Conroy notes that 'Watson does not budge in the actual telling from a strict present-tense point of view'[22] – that is, he never foreshadows crucial details despite knowing them at the time of writing. Conroy sums up the difficult balancing act neatly: 'Watson's narrative problem is simultaneously to give the reader access to all the information Holmes has and yet to ensure that he will fail to analyze it correctly.'[23]

Watson's own personality may shape our understanding and appreciation of his more famous colleague, yet he often stifles his own responses in order to show Holmes at work without drawing attention to himself as the lens through which we observe. Though he may often provide an emotional context to Holmes's calm deductions, if Holmes can be characterised as a 'calculating machine', Watson at times behaves simply as a 'recording machine'. I've enjoyed redressing this by allowing more insight into Watson's thought processes, refusing to let him hide behind his friend. Importantly, while I've indulged myself in exploring Watson's insecurities, jealousies and personal life, I have no compulsion to study Holmes to any similar degree – my instinct is that he must remain at arm's length.

---

22   Conroy, Peter, 'The Importance of Being Watson', in Orel, p.43.

23   Ibid., p.48.

Evoking Conan Doyle's written style

The final aspect of creating a 'faithful' pastiche is perhaps the most demanding, and the most crucial. It's all very well to understand a little about the required tone of a Holmes story, and the shape of the plot and the behaviour of the participants – but when it comes to putting fingers to computer keys (another anachronism at odds with Conan Doyle!), a pastiche-writer must of course decide which words to use. Echoing Pierre Menard again, I was not to become Conan Doyle, so instead I would have to mimic his style through close observation.

As far as I can tell, there are few detailed analyses of Conan Doyle's writing style. Most critics dispense of the subject with a single comment, usually derogatory, or at best a backhanded compliment. For example, Kim Herzinger states, 'Even in the best of the stories, Conan Doyle's writing achieves a kind of laughable mediocrity,' then goes on to note that readers rarely have cause to examine the prose closely, as 'To do so would be to have our pleasure checked by the awful claims of aesthetic principle and to disallow the kind of indulgence Holmes deserves.'[24] Conan Doyle himself was downbeat about his literary achievements:

> The best literary work is that which leaves the reader better for having read it. Now, nobody can possibly be the better – in the high sense in which I mean it – for reading Sherlock Holmes, although he may have passed

---

24   Herzinger, pp.104–05.

a pleasant hour in doing so. It was not to my mind high work, and no detective work ever can be, apart from the fact that all work dealing with criminal matters is a cheap way of rousing the interest of the reader.[25]

John Le Carré turns this same sentiment into a far more positive statement, and goes on to note that simple language allows Holmes stories to be translated easily into practically any language, a crucial aspect to the popularity of Conan Doyle's stories the world over:

> Peek up Conan Doyle's sleeve and you will at first be disappointed; no fine turns of phrase, no clever adjectives that leap off the page, no arresting psychological insights. Instead, what you are looking at is a kind of narrative perfection; a perfect interplay between dialogue and description, perfect characterisation and perfect timing.[26]

My own analysis was quantitative rather than qualitative. Some findings merely satisfied my curiosity – for example, there are eight instances of 'elementary' in the canon, and eighty-two instances of 'my dear Watson', though none of those (as we know) in conjunction with 'elementary'. But what of the finding that there are fifty-three instances of the word

---

25   Conan Doyle, in *Tit-Bits*.

26   Le Carré, John, in Klinger, Leslie S., *The New Annotated Sherlock Holmes, Volume I*, Introduction, p.xiii.

'deduction' and thirty-six of 'deduce', out of a total word count of almost 660,000 words? That seems to suggest a degree of talking *around* Holmes's greatest skill rather than referring to it directly.

Some of the most useful findings from my analysis relate to plainer details. Contractions appear relatively infrequently (154 instances of 'I've' versus 1,463 'I have'), with some exceptions (470 instances of 'don't' as opposed to 225 'do not'). In keeping with critical assessments of Conan Doyle's style as lacking in floridity, dialogue tags are almost always simply 'said', with 3,104 instances of that verb as opposed to 190 'remarked' or 21 'uttered' – and the much-mocked dialogue tag 'ejaculated' appears only 14 times in total. Similarly, there are few adverbs applied to speech, the most frequent being the perfectly functional 'quietly' (52 instances). There are no instances of 'irritably', an adverb that is frequently applied in Holmesian pastiches. A broader observation is that Conan Doyle can often be accused of the modern creative-writing bugbear of 'telling rather than showing', as in 'Our acquaintance looked surprised', though he is also adept at supporting characters' stated emotions through their actions: '"At eight o'clock," she said, gulping in her throat to keep down her agitation.'

All of this is useful ammunition, but of course judgement calls are required in order to fulfil the expectations of the 'implied reader'. Some readers of a modern Holmes pastiche novel will never have read Conan Doyle, but will instead have grown up with the pop-culture image of Holmes and Watson in films and TV series, so it is tone and character that are likely to chime with their expectations. Mysteries must be more devious than in many of the canonical tales, in order to match the complexity of plots in multi-episodic HBO or Netflix thrillers. Some stylistic aspects of the canonical tales may be jarring and must be weighed up by the pastiche-writer. For example, how might modern readers respond to Conan Doyle's tendency to go to town on colloquialisms and accents, as in, 'It hain't got no fangs, so I gives it the run o' the room, for it keeps the bettles down'?[27]

The limits of 'literary forgery'

So: the writing of a Holmesian – or any – pastiche is a careful balancing act, negotiating the necessary and the optional, the familiar and new elements. As in forty of the fifty-six canonical short stories, my three Sherlock Holmes novels take place in cold weather (if it's not bad weather, the weather is rarely described at all in the original stories). Many aspects of Victoriana are amped up in order to adhere to perceived modern expectations of the era, largely informed by popular culture. My novel *The Twelve Thefts of Christmas* draws as much upon the influence of the Victorian era on modern festive celebrations as if does upon Conan Doyle's work; there is only one Holmes story, 'The Blue Carbuncle', that relates indirectly to Christmastime, yet Sherlock Holmes and Victorian Christmases seem so suited to one another that many people are likely to consider them established bedfellows. Finally, my analysis

---
27   Conan Doyle, Arthur, *The Sign of Four*, p.61.

of Conan Doyle's writing style informed many aspects of the style I deployed, such as the hyphenation of 'to-day', which I felt evoked a certain tone without an impact on the flow of sentences, whereas some hallmarks were abandoned – for example, Conan Doyle much prefers the word order 'said he' to 'he said', but I considered that the former would present an unconscious obstacle to modern readers.

In truth, the expectations of my own 'implied reader' are merely *my* assumptions about *their* assumptions. Like Pierre Menard, it would be possible to follow this spiral of guesswork to an absurd end and produce a slavish copy of little interest to the general reader, or alternatively a mishmash of pop-culture images bearing no direct relation to Arthur Conan Doyle's work. My strong feeling is that a writer as popular and populist as Conan Doyle, and a character as beloved as Sherlock Holmes, deserve pastiches that are respectful to the precedents that have been established but which, far more importantly, remain in the same spirit.

* * *

Once our visitor had departed, I turned to face Sherlock Holmes.

'Now that we are alone, I insist that you explain your methods to me,' I said.

My friend raised an eyebrow. 'Must I? Or do you simply *expect* me to do so?'

I did nothing to hide my irritation. 'Either way, Holmes.

The type of carriage, the appearance of the lad, his clean-shaven face, this wooden crate—' I pointed to that same object upon the dinner table, still covered with brown paper. 'It is unfathomable how you could have read all that simply in the sound of his approach.'

'Good,' Holmes said simply.

'Good? Are you to leave it at that?'

'I merely encourage you to develop your postulation.'

I stared at him. 'I have no postulation! All I said was that it was impossible.'

Holmes raised a finger as if in warning. 'The word you used was "unfathomable".'

'Indeed. Now I raise my earlier bid. Your accomplishment was impossible.'

My friend smiled, and a more aggravating expression I have never known.

I groaned as realisation dawned upon me. '"When you have eliminated the impossible, whatever remains, however improbable, must be the truth."' I recited this pronouncement like a dull schoolchild, which reflected my mood accurately enough.

'So, then?'

'You performed no deduction at all. Instead, you…' I paused, searching for the answer. 'You simply knew that the boy was coming here.'

Holmes bowed his head. 'That young fellow was Dobson junior, from the bakery on Hereford Road. I know him by sight, having performed a trivial service for his father. When

I called in yesterday afternoon to provide the summary of my findings, Dobson senior was insistent that he would demonstrate his thanks in lieu of the payment I refused. The son performs all deliveries via his gig, and deploys wooden crates for large or fragile loads.'

I shook my head in dismay as I pulled away the paper from the crate to reveal an array of pastries and tarts, along with provisions including bacon and a brace of eggs. Nestled alongside these lay a bottle of decent brandy.

'You may instruct Mrs Hudson to serve you any or all of it,' Holmes said, turning away. 'I have no appetite myself.'

My stomach growled as I looked upon the food.

'It is a shame,' I said, without having intended to speak my thoughts aloud.

'What is?'

'That your deductive feat was a fraud. I am at a loss as to how to begin the tale I have been attempting to compose, and a demonstration of your powers would have been an apt beginning.'

Holmes's eyes gleamed. 'I have not read all of your accounts of my cases, but I have seen enough of them to know that you are accustomed to taking liberties. I trust you will do so again.'

I presumed I was being chastised. It was true that I had exerted a degree of editorial power over my accounts. I had begun to prepare a defence when Holmes interrupted my thoughts.

'I will not stand in your way,' he said.

I hesitated. 'Then you are not offended by the alterations I make?'

Holmes laughed, an occurrence rare enough that it is one of those aspects of my friend's character that I frequently omit from my accounts.

'Not in the least,' he said amiably. 'Watson, as my biographer you may marry me, murder me, or do anything you like with me. I assure you that nothing you do to me in your tales will cause me the least harm.'

Sources

It Bleeds

Ayatsuji, Yukito, *The Decagon House Murders* (Locked Room International, 2015)

Christie, Agatha, *Murder on the Orient Express* (Collins Crime Club, 1934)

Eco, Umberto, *Six Walks in the Fictional Woods* (Harvard University Press, 1994)

Knox, Father Ronald & H. Harrington (eds), *The Best English Detective Stories of 1928* (Horace Liveright, 1929)

Yokomizo, Seishi, *The Honjin Murders* (Pushkin Press, 2019)

The Killer Inside Me: Writing the Criminal

Thompson, Jim, *The Getaway* (Signet, 1958)

Thompson, Jim, *The Grifters* (Regency Books, 1963)

Thompson, Jim, *Pop. 1280* (Gold Medal Books, 1964)

Thompson, Jim, *Savage Night* (Lion Books, 1953)

Thompson, Jim, *The Killer Inside Me* (Fawcett Publications, 1952)

The Deader the Better: On Writing the Murder

Adair, Gilbert, *The Death of the Novel* (Heinemann, 1992)

Auden, W.H., 'The Guilty Vicarage' (*Harper's Magazine*, 1948)

Auster, Paul, *City of Glass* (Sun & Moon Press, 1985)

Binet, Laurent, *The 7th Function of Language* (Farrar, Straus and Giroux, 2017)

Borges, Jorge Luis, 'Death and the Compass' (*Sur*, 1942)

Camus, Albert, *The Just Assassins* (Gallimard, 1949)

Chandler, Raymond, *The Lady in the Lake* (Alfred A. Knopf, 1943)

Chandler, Raymond, 'The Simple Act of Murder' (*Atlantic Monthly*, 1944)

Chesterton, G.K., 'The Blue Cross' (*Saturday Evening Post*, 1910)

De Quincey, Thomas, 'On Murder Considered as One of the Fine Arts' (*Blackwood's Magazine*, 1827)

Dine, SS. Van – 'Twenty Rules for Writing Detective Fiction' (*American Magazine*, 1928)

Dostoevsky, Fyodor, *Crime and Punishment* (1866)

Doyle, Arthur Conan, *The Sign of the Four* (*Lippincott's Magazine*, 1890)

Ellis, Bret Easton, *American Psycho* (Vintage, 1991)

Foucault, Michel, 'What is an Author?' (*Bulletin de la Société Française de Philosophic*, 1969)

Gide, André, *The Vatican Cellars* (Penguin, 1914)

Greenlaw, Lavinia, *Some Answers Without Questions* (Faber, 2021)

Hamilton, Patrick, *Rope* (1929)

Highsmith, Patricia, *The Talented Mr Ripley* (Cresset Press, 1955)

Iles, Francis, *Malice Aforethought* (Gollancz, 1931)

Kafka, Franz, *The Trial* (Verlag Die Schmiede, 1925)

Perec, Georges, *Life: A User's Manual* (Hachette, 1978)

Poe, Edgar Allan, 'The Murders in the Rue Morgue' (*Graham's Magazine*, 1841)

Poe, Edgar Allan, 'The Murder of Marie Rogêt' (*Snowden's Ladies' Companion*, 1842–43)

Pynchon, Thomas, *The Crying of Lot 49* (J.B. Lippincott & Co., 1965)

Robbe-Grillet, Alain, *The Erasers* (1953)

Sartre, Jean-Paul, *Dirty Hands* (1948)

Wilde, Oscar, 'Pen, Pencil, and Poison: A Study in Green' (*Fortnightly Review*, 1885)

No Compromises: The Crime Fiction of Patricia Highsmith

Highsmith, Patricia, *Ripley Under Ground* (Heinemann, 1970)

Highsmith, Patricia, *Strangers on a Train* (Harper & Brothers, 1950)

Highsmith, Patricia, *A Suspension of Mercy* (Heinemann, 1965)

Highsmith, Patricia, *The Talented Mr Ripley* (Cresset Press, 1955)

There's Been a Murder: Miscarriages of Justice, Respectability and the Fatal Flaw

Godwin, William, *Things as They Are; or, The Adventures of Caleb Williams* (1794)

Grisham, John, *The Firm* (Random House, 1991)

House, Jack, *Square Mile of Murder, Horrific Glasgow Killings* (Black & White Publishing, 1961)

Roughead, William, *The Trial of Oscar Slater* (1910)

On Reading as Escape: All of Christie's Murderers, and Me

Christia, Agatha, *The Mysterious Affair at Styles* (John Lane, 1920)

Making the Dead Dance: Historical Crime Fiction

Clavell, James, *Shōgun* (Hodder & Stoughton, 1975)

Eco, Umberto, *The Name of the Rose* (Harcourt, 1980)

Faulks, Sebastian, *Birdsong* (Hutchinson, 1993)

Seth, Vikram, *A Suitable Boy* (Phoenix House, 1993)

The Method and the Effect: Conjuring the Impossible Crime

Adey, Robert, *Locked Room Murders* (Crossover Press, 1991)

Amis, Kingsley, *Times Literary Supplement*, 6 June 1981

Brean, Herbert, *Wilders Walk Away* (William Morrow, 1948)

Carr, John Dickson, 'The Grandest Game in the World' in *The Door to Doom, and Other Detections* (Harper & Row, 1980) (Essay originally published 1963)

Carr, John Dickson, *The Hollow Man* (Hamish Hamilton, 1935)

Edwards, Martin, *The Life of Crime* (Harper Collins, 2022)

Greene, Douglas G., *The Man Who Explained Miracles* (Otto Penzler Books, 1995)

Lamont, Peter and Wiseman, Richard, *Magic in Theory: An Introduction to the Theoretical and Psychological Elements of Conjuring* (University of Hertfordshire Press, 1999)

Macknik, Stephen and Martinez-Conde, Susana, with Blakeslee, Sandra, *Sleights of Mind: What the Neuroscience of Magic Reveals about Our Everyday Deceptions* (Profile Books, 2010)

Penzler, Otto (ed.), *The Black Lizard Big Book of Locked-Room Mysteries* (Vintage Crime/Black Lizard, 2014)

Sacks, Oliver, 'What hallucination reveals about our minds' (TED Talk, 2009)

Sacks, Oliver, *Musicophilia: Tales of Music and the Brain* (Pan Macmillan, 2011)

Taylor, Robert Lewis, 'John Dickson Carr' (*New Yorker*, 8 September 1951)

The Problem of the Faithful Pastiche

Borges, Jorge Luis, *Labyrinths* (Penguin, 1970)

Conan Doyle, Arthur, *Memories and Adventures* (Little, Brown, 1924)

Lellenberg, Jon, Daniel Stashower & Charles Foley (eds), *Arthur Conan Doyle: A Life in Letters* (HarperPress, 2007)

Orel, Harold, *Critical Essays on Sir Arthur Conan Doyle* (G.K. Hall & Co., 1992)

Further Reading

As with the previous two volumes in this series, the following lists of recommended texts are not intended to form an exhaustive bibliography in the field of mystery and crime writing. Instead, we've tried to compile a reading list which provides breadth and comprehension for those looking to educate themselves further in the genre, as well as some of the cornerstones of contemporary crime writing. Some of the titles recommended here are already well-known classics, and will feature on many readers' bookshelves; others are relatively unknown.

Hopefully these suggestions provide a helpful reading list for both the rookie crime reader and the seasoned veteran.

100 Mystery Novels
1. Voltaire – *Zadig* (1747)
2. Wilkie Collins – *The Woman in White* (1860)
3. Charles Felix – *The Notting Hill Mystery* (1865)
4. Fyodor Dostoevsky – *Crime and Punishment* (1866)
5. Wilkie Collins – *The Moonstone* (1868)
6. Robert Louis Stevenson – *The Strange Case of Dr Jekyll and Mr Hyde* (1886)
7. Arthur Conan Doyle – *The Hound of the Baskervilles* (1902)

8. Anna Katharine Green – *The Amethyst Box* (1905)
9. Gaston Leroux – *The Mystery of the Yellow Room* (1907)
10. A.A. Milne – *The Red House Mystery* (1922)
11. Dorothy L. Sayers – *Whose Body?* (1923)
12. Agatha Christie – *The Murder of Roger Ackroyd* (1926)
13. Gladys Mitchell – *Speedy Death* (1929)
14. Dashiell Hammett – *The Maltese Falcon* (1930)
15. Francis Iles – *Malice Aforethought* (1931)
16. Georges Simenon – *The Madman of Bergerac* (1932)
17. Ellery Queen – *The Egyptian Cross Mystery* (1932)
18. Rudolph Fisher – *The Conjure Man Dies* (1932)
19. Freeman Wills Crofts – *The Hog's Back Mystery* (1933)
20. Ngaio Marsh – *A Man Lay Dead* (1934)
21. James M. Cain – *The Postman Always Rings Twice* (1934)
22. Nigel Strangeways – *A Question of Proof* (1935)
23. John Dickson Carr – *The Hollow Man* (1935)
24. E.C. Bentley – *Trent's Last Case* (1936)
25. Michael Innes – *Hamlet, Revenge!* (1937)
26. Ernest Borneman – *The Face on the Cutting Room Floor* (1937)
27. Graham Greene – *Brighton Rock* (1938)
28. Nicholas Blake – *The Beast Must Die* (1938)
29. Daphne Du Maurier – *Rebecca* (1938)
30. Raymond Chandler – *The Big Sleep* (1939)
31. Eric Ambler – *The Mask of Dimitrios* (1939)
32. Agatha Christie – *And Then There Were None* (1939)
33. Cornell Woolrich – *The Bride Wore Black* (1940)
34. Raymond Chandler – *Farewell, My Lovely* (1940)
35. Patrick Hamilton – *Hangover Square* (1941)

36. George Bellairs – *The Dead Shall be Raised* (1942)
37. Albert Camus – *L'Etranger* (1942)
38. Graham Greene – *The Ministry of Fear* (1943)
39. E.R.C. Lorac – *Fell Murder* (1944)
40. Joel Townsley Rogers – *The Red Right Hand* (1945)
41. Seishi Yokomizo – *The Honjin Murders* (1946)
42. Edmund Crispin – *The Moving Toyshop* (1946)
43. Dorothy B. Hughes – *In a Lonely Place* (1947)
44. Josephine Tey – *The Franchise Affair* (1948)
45. Christianna Brand – *Death of Jezebel* (1948)
46. Ross Macdonald – *The Moving Target* (1949)
47. Helen McCloy – *Through a Glass, Darkly* (1950)
48. Josephine Tey – *The Daughter of Time* (1951)
49. Cyril Hare – *An English Murder* (1951)
50. Margery Allingham – *The Tiger in the Smoke* (1952)
51. Jim Thompson – *The Killer Inside Me* (1952)
52. Boileau-Narcejac – *She Who Was No More* (1952)
53. Ira Levin – *A Kiss Before Dying* (1953)
54. Patricia Highsmith – *The Talented Mr Ripley* (1955)
55. Margaret Millar – *Beast in View* (1955)
56. Christianna Brand – *Tour de Force* (1955)
57. Celia Fremlin – *Uncle Paul* (1959)
58. Julian Symonds – *The Progress of a Crime* (1960)
59. Charles Willeford – *Cockfighter* (1962)
60. Chester Himes – *Cotton Comes to Harlem* (1964)
61. Colin Dexter – *Last Seen Wearing* (1976)
62. Ellis Peters – *A Morbid Taste for Bones* (1977)
63. Ruth Rendell – *A Judgement in Stone* (1977)

64. Umberto Eco – *The Name of the Rose* (1980)
65. Mark Behm – *The Eye of the Beholder* (1980)
66. Thomas Harris – *Red Dragon* (1981)
67. Soji Shimada – *The Tokyo Zodiac Murders* (1981)
68. Barbara Vine – *A Dark-Adapted Eye* (1986)
69. James Ellroy – *The Black Dahlia* (1987)
70. Yukito Ayatsuji – *The Decagon House Murders* (1987)
71. Celia Dale – *Sheep's Clothing* (1988)
72. Philip Kerr – *March Violets* (1989)
73. James Lee Burke – *Black Cherry Blues* (1989)
74. Elmore Leonard – *Get Shorty* (1990)
75. Derek Raymond – *I Was Dora Suarez* (1990)
76. Bret Easton Ellis – *American Psycho* (1991)
77. Peter Hoeg – *Miss Smilia's Feeling for Snow* (1992)
78. Donna Tartt – *The Secret History* (1992)
79. Val McDermid – *The Mermaids Singing* (1995)
80. Mike Phillips – *The Dancing Face* (1997)
81. Irvine Welsh – *Filth* (1998)
82. Jake Arnott – *The Long Firm* (1999)
83. Kazuo Ishiguro – *When We Were Orphans* (2000)
84. David Peace – *Nineteen Seventy-Seven* (2000)
85. Dennis Lehane – *Mystic River* (2001)
86. Sarah Waters – *Fingersmith* (2002)
87. Louise Welsh – *The Cutting Room* (2002)
88. C.J. Sansom – *Dissolution* (2003)
89. Ian Rankin – *The Naming of the Dead* (2005)
90. Peter Temple – *The Broken Shore* (2005)
91. Stieg Larsson – *The Girl with the Dragon Tattoo* (2005)

92. Tom Franklin – *Crooked Letter, Crooked Letter* (2010)
93. S.J. Parris – *Heresy* (2010)
94. Alice Thompson – *The Existential Detective* (2010)
95. Ray Celestin – *The Axeman's Jazz* (2014)
96. Ottessa Moshfegh – *Eileen* (2015)
97. Leila Slimani – *Lullaby* (2016)
98. Abir Mukherjee – *A Rising Man* (2016)
99. Oyinkan Braithwaite – *My Sister, the Serial Killer* (2018)
100. Stuart Turton – *The Devil and the Dark Water* (2020)

50 Mystery Short Stories

1. E.T.A. Hoffmann – 'Mademoiselle de Scuderi' (1819)
2. J. Sheridan Le Fanu – 'A Passage in the Secret History of an Irish Countess' (1838)
3. Edgar Allan Poe – 'The Murders in the Rue Morgue' (1841)
4. Wilkie Collins – 'A Terribly Strange Bed' (1852)
5. Mary E. Braddon – 'The Mystery at Fernwood' (1862)
6. Jules Barbey d'Aurevilly – 'The Crimson Curtain' (1866)
7. Robert Louis Stevenson – 'Markheim' (1885)
8. Arthur Conan Doyle – 'The Red Headed League' (1891)
9. Arthur Conan Doyle – 'The Speckled Band' (1892)
10. E.W. Hornung – 'The Ides of March' (1898)
11. Maurice Leblanc – 'The Arrest of Arsene Lupin' (1905)
12. Maurice Leblanc – 'Arsene Lupin in Prison' (1905)
13. Jacques Futrelle – 'The Problem of Cell 13' (1905)
14. G.K. Chesteron – 'The Blue Cross' (1910)
15. William Hope Hodgson – 'The Whistling Room' (1910)
16. G.K. Chesteron – 'The Secret Garden' (1911)

17. Mary Roberts Rinehart – 'Locked Doors' (1914)
18. Susan Glaspell – 'A Jury of Her Peers' (1917)
19. Agatha Christie – 'The Adventure of the Egyptian Tomb' (1923)
20. Dashiell Hammett – 'The House in Turk Street' (1924)
21. Richard Connell – 'The Most Dangerous Game' (1924)
22. Agatha Christie – 'Witness for the Prosecution' (1925)
23. Ernest Hemingway – 'The Killers' (1927)
24. Dorothy L. Sayers – 'Murder at Pentecost' (1933)
25. Raymond Chandler – 'Blackmailers Don't Shoot' (1933)
26. John Dickson Carr – 'The Wrong Problem' (1936)
27. Graham Greene – 'The Case for the Defence' (1939)
28. Jorge Luis Borges – 'Death and the Compass' (1942)
29. Ray Bradbury – 'The Fruit at the Bottom of the Bowl' (1948)
30. Clayton Rawson – 'From Another World' (1948)
31. Lord Dunsany – 'The Two Bottles of Relish' (1952)
32. Roald Dahl – 'Lamb to the Slaughter' (1953)
33. Flannery O'Connor – 'A Good Man is Hard to Find' (1953)
34. Michael Innes – 'The Furies' (1954)
35. Margery Allingham – 'Bluebeard's Bathtub' (1955)
36. Joyce Carol Oates – 'Where Are You Going, Where Have You Been?' (1966)
37. Edward D. Hoch – 'The Oblong Room' (1967)
38. Stanley Ellin – 'The Last Bottle in the World' (1968)
39. Robert Barnard – 'Death of an Old Goat' (1974)
40. Roald Dahl – 'The Hitch-Hiker' (1977)
41. Nadine Gordimer – 'Country Lovers' (1980)
42. Patricia Highsmith – 'The Terror of Basket-Weaving' (1981)

43. Ruth Rendell – 'Long Live the Queen' (1991)
44. Sara Paretsky – 'Grace Notes' (1995)
45. Ruth Rendell – 'Blood Lines' (1995)
46. Ian Rankin – 'Death is Not the End' (1998)
47. Henning Mankell – 'The Man on the Beach' (1999)
48. Minette Walters – 'The Tinder Box' (2005)
49. George Saunders – 'Victory Lap' (2009)
50. Minette Walters – 'Chickenfeed' (2013)

About the Authors

Quentin Bates has roots in Iceland that lie very deep. In addition to his own fiction, he has translated some of Iceland's coolest writers into English.

Paul Finch is an ex-cop and journalist turned bestselling author. He first cut his literary teeth penning episodes of the TV drama *The Bill*, and has written extensively in the horror, fantasy and historical epic genres, including for *Doctor Who*. However, he is best known for his crime/thriller novels, of which there are twelve to date, including the Heckenburg and Clayburn series with HarperCollins (the first Lucy Clayburn novel, *Strangers*, making the *Sunday Times* Top 10) and two stand-alones with Orion. Paul lives in Lancashire with his wife and business partner, Cathy. Website: paulfinch-writer.blogspot.com/.

Barry Forshaw is a leading UK expert on crime fiction and film. He is the *Financial Times*' crime fiction critic, and his books include *Crime Fiction: A Reader's Guide*, the Keating Award-winning *Brit Noir* (plus *Nordic, American, Euro* and *Historical Noir*). His other work includes *British Gothic Cinema, Italian Cinema, Simenon: The Man, The Books, The Films, Sex* *and Film, Film Noir, British Crime Writing: An Encyclopedia* (also a Keating winner), *Death in a Cold Climate* and *Stieg Larsson: The Man Who Left Too Soon*. He edits *DVD Choice* and *Crime Time* (www.crimetime.co.uk) and provides many Blu-ray booklets and commentaries.

Andrew Gallix is an Anglo-French writer and occasional translator, who teaches at the Sorbonne and edits *3:AM Magazine*. His books include *Unwords* (Dodo Ink, 2024) and *We'll Never Have Paris* (Repeater Books, 2019) alongside *Love Bites: Fiction Inspired by Pete Shelley* (Dostoyevsky Wannabe, 2019) and *Punk is Dead: Modernity Killed Every Night* (Zero Books, 2017) which he co-edited. *Loren Ipsum*, his debut novel, will be published by Dodo Ink. His website is andrewgallix.com and he tweets @andrewgallix.

Jessie Greengrass is the author of two novels: *The High House*, which was shortlisted for the Costa Novel Prize 2021, the Orwell Prize for Political Fiction 2022 and the Encore Award 2022, and *Sight*, which was published in 2018 and shortlisted for the 2018 Women's Prize for Fiction. Her collection of short stories, *An Account of the Decline of the Great Auk, According to One Who Saw It* was published in 2015. It won the Edge Hill Prize 2016, a Somerset Maugham Award, and was shortlisted for the *Sunday Times* PFD Young Writer of the Year Award.

Charlie Higson is an author, actor, producer, comedian and writer for TV, film and radio. Both his *Young Bond* and *The*

Enemy series for teenagers have sold over a million copies in the UK. The rights to *The Enemy* books have been sold to a leading US studio who are currently developing it as a major movie franchise. Charlie wrote four adult crime novels, *King of the Ants*, *Happy Now*, *Full Whack* and *Getting Rid of Mr Kitchen* in the 1990s and returned to crime writing in 2022 with the publication of *Whatever Gets You Through the Night*. 2023 saw his first foray into adult James Bond novels with *On His Majesty's Secret Service*, published to coincide with the coronation of King Charles III. His book for younger children, *Worst. Holiday. Ever*, was published in 2021, with the sequel, *Worst. Superhero. Ever*, out in the autumn 2024. TV writing work includes *Saturday Live*, *Harry Enfield's Television Programme*, *Agatha Christie's Miss Marple*, *Professor Branestawm*, the sitcom *Swiss Toni*, and the BAFTA-winning sketch show *The Fast Show*, which he co-created, co-produced and starred in with Paul Whitehouse. Charlie and Paul co-produced and performed in the award-winning spoof radio series *Down the Line* for BBC Radio 4, which led to the BBC2 television series *Bellamy's People*. Charlie was also show-runner and lead writer on two drama series – *Randall & Hopkirk Deceased*, for the BBC, and *Jekyll & Hyde*, for ITV. As well as appearing in many of his own productions, Charlie had major acting roles in the dramas *Broadchurch* and *Grantchester* in 2017. In 2023 Charlie launched his own podcast, a history of the British monarchy called *Willy Willy Harry Stee*.

Carole Johnstone grew up in Lanarkshire, Scotland, and in her twenties relocated to Essex to work in medical physics. She has been writing as long as she can remember and is an award-winning short story writer. Her debut novel, *Mirrorland*, a gothic suspense set in Edinburgh, described by Stephen King as 'Dark and devious, beautifully written and plotted with a watchmaker's precision', has been optioned for TV, with translation rights sold to 14 other territories. Her second novel, *The Blackhouse*, an unusual murder-mystery set in the Outer Hebrides, was published in 2022. She now writes full-time and lives with her husband in the West Highlands, although her heart belongs to the sea and the wild islands of the Outer Hebrides.

Vaseem Khan is the author of two award-winning crime series set in India, the *Baby Ganesh Agency* series set in modern Mumbai, and the *Malabar House* historical crime novels set in 1950s Bombay. His first book, *The Unexpected Inheritance of Inspector Chopra*, was selected by the *Sunday Times* as one of the 40 best crime novels published 2015–2020, and is translated into 17 languages. In 2021, *Midnight at Malabar House* won the Crime Writers Association Historical Dagger. Vaseem was born in England, but spent a decade working in India. In 2023, Vaseem was elected the first non-white Chair of the 70-year-old UK Crime Writers Association.

Tess Little is a writer, historian, and Fellow of All Souls College, University of Oxford. Her essays, criticism, and short stories have appeared in various places, including *The White Review*, *Literary Review*, *CrimeReads*, *The Mays Anthology*, and on posters outside a London tube station. Her debut novel *The Octopus* was first published in 2020; it has since been published as *The Ninth Guest* in the UK and *The Last Guest* in the US.

Tim Major is a writer and freelance editor from York. His books include three Sherlock Holmes novels – *The Back to Front Murder*, *The Defaced Men* and *The Twelve Thefts of Christmas* – as well as *Jekyll & Hyde: Consulting Detectives*, short story collection *And the House Lights Dim* and a monograph about the 1915 silent crime film, *Les Vampires*. Tim's short stories have been selected for *Best of British Science Fiction*, *Best of British Fantasy* and *Best Horror of the Year*. Find out more at www.timjmajor.com.

Tom Mead is a Derbyshire mystery writer and aficionado of Golden Age crime fiction. His debut novel, *Death and the Conjuror*, was an international bestseller, nominated for several awards, and named one of the best mysteries of the year by *The Guardian* and *Publishers Weekly*. Its sequel, *The Murder Wheel*, was described as 'pure nostalgic pleasure' by the *Wall Street Journal* and 'a delight' by the *Daily Mail*. It was also named one of the Best Traditional Mysteries of 2023 by *Crimereads*. His third novel, *Cabaret Macabre*, will be published in 2024.

Saima Mir is an award-winning journalist and writer. Her novel *The Khan* was published in 2021 and its sequel, *Vengeance*, in 2024. Her awards include the Commonwealth Broadcasting Association Worldview Award, and the K. Blundell Trust

Award. She has written for *The Guardian*, *The Times*, *The Independent* and the *Daily Telegraph*, and worked for the BBC.

Louise Welsh is the author of ten novels including *The Cutting Room*, the *Plague Times* trilogy and *To the Dogs*. Louise has a ten-year practice in opera with composer Stuart MacRae. Their most recent opera, *Anthropocene*, originally commissioned by Scottish Opera, has enjoyed productions in the UK, Germany and Salzberg. She was co-director (with Jude Barber) of the Empire Café, an award-winning exploration of Scotland's relationship with the North Atlantic slave trade. She has received numerous awards and international fellowships, including honorary doctorates from Napier University and the Open University. Louise is Professor of Creative Writing at University of Glasgow and a Fellow of the Royal Society of Edinburgh and the Royal Society of Literature.

About the Editors

Dan Coxon is an award-winning editor and writer based in London. He has been a finalist for the Shirley Jackson Awards and the British Fantasy Awards (six times), with *Writing the Uncanny* (co-edited with Richard V. Hirst) winning the British Fantasy Award for Best Non-Fiction 2022. His anthology *Being Dad* won a Saboteur Award in 2016. His short stories have appeared in various anthologies and magazines, including *Shakespeare Unleashed*, *Beyond the Veil*, *Fiends in the Furrows III* and *Great British Horror 7: Major Arcana*. His latest fiction anthology – *For Tomorrow* – was published by Black Shuck Books in March 2023.

Richard V. Hirst is a writer and editor from Preston. His writing has been published in *The Guardian*, the *Big Issue*, *Time Out* and others.

About Dead Ink

Dead Ink is a publisher of bold new fiction based in Liverpool. We're an Arts Council England National Portfolio Organisation.

If you would like to keep up to date with what we're up to, check out our website and join our mailing list.

www.deadinkbooks.com | @deadinkbooks